11/17/95

To Ruth

For your continued study of this subject.

Happy Birthday.

Love,

Gloria

A Transported Life:
Memories of Kindertransport

Thea Feliks Eden, Tel Aviv, Israel, February 1953

The Oral History of Thea Feliks Eden

Edited by Irene Reti and Valerie Jean Chase

Printed in the United States of America by McNaughton and Gunn.

Library of Congress Cataloging-in-Publication Data
Eden, Thea, 1926-1994.
A transported life: memories of Kindertransport: the oral history of Thea Eden / edited by Irene Reti and Valerie Jean Chase.
p.   cm.
Includes bibliographical references.

ISBN 0-939821-07-9

1. Eden, Thea. 1926-1994—Childhood and youth. 2. Jews—Germany—Cologne—Biography. 3. Refugees, Jewish—England—Biography. 4. Holocaust, Jewish (1939-1945)—Personal narratives. 5. Zbaszyn (Poland: Concentration camp) 6. World War, 1939-1945—Jews—Rescue—Poland. 7. Cologne (Germany)—Ethnic relations. I. Reti, Irene, 1961— . II. Chase, Valerie Jean, 1957— . III. Title.
DS135.G5E319 1995
940.53'161—dc20
[B]   94-48731
                                                              CIP

Acknowledgements:
Deepest thanks to Ilana Eden for her support of this book. Input from the following people was also invaluable: Randall Jarrell, Benno Katz, Mary Stoddard, and Deborah Turner. And the greatest appreciation to Julia Chapin for her editorial support.

Fifty percent of the net proceeds from each sale of this book will be donated to an organization which works to preserve the memories of Holocaust survivors through oral history.

Cover Photograph: Leopold and Thea Feliks, Zbaszyn, Poland, 1939

Dedicated to
Chaya Messer Feliks

Zbaszyn, Poland, 1939

CONTENTS

List of Photographs

Historical Introduction

As the millennium approaches, the number of Holocaust survivors dwindles each year. I can begin to imagine a time when there will be no one left to tell the story, to say, "I was there and this is how it was." We who were not there are challenged to listen deeply, to carry the stories of the survivors into the future. For we are the ones who one day may be called upon to say, "I was not there, but I knew many who were. And this is what they said."

Each individual's experience of the Holocaust was different, a reflection of geography, family history, chance, circumstance, age, health, and a myriad of other factors. For those of us who were not there, who seek to somehow comprehend the events of the Holocaust, each of these stories becomes a vital link in understanding a kaleidoscope of atrocity.

While numerous oral histories of Holocaust survivors have been collected for archives and publications all over the world, few of these accounts have come from those who were children at the time. As Julie Heifetz writes in her book, *Too Young to Remember*:[1]

> Child survivors have been disregarded as reliable
> sources of information. Researchers have not sought
> out child survivors, instead interviewing important
> people, leaders whose perceptions and memories
> they trust more than those of children.

This book is the oral history of Thea Feliks Eden, child survivor of the Holocaust. It defies the assumption that child survivors were "too young to remember," that they could somehow erase their past and start new lives in new lands after the war, carefree lives, lives unmarked by the terror and degradation they experienced as Jewish children under the Nazi regime. The stunning detail and clarity of this manuscript is testament to the fallacy of that assumption. Thea did remember. She remembered in vivid, heartbreaking detail. She remembered growing up in Nazi Cologne, passing public bulletin boards plastered with Nazi propaganda posters featuring brutal caricatures of Jews, the posters protected behind chicken wire so no one could remove them. She remembered Nazis chasing her through endless streets and her terror even inside her house, where a Nazi tenant boarded on one of the floors because her widowed mother needed the money. And she remembered the day a Nazi threw a rock at her eye and she thought her eye was running out into her hand there was so much blood. All her life she dreamt of stormtroopers, "being able to walk through doors whether you locked them or not."

She remembered Zbaszyn,[2] the internment camp where women died in abandoned horse stalls, children picked lice out of each other's hair, and the latrines were long trenches filled with rats and disease. She remembered the Kindertransport, 96 terrified children on the last boat out of Gdynia before war broke out. And she remembered the years in England when the refugee children were told to be merry, not to cry in front of anyone because no one wanted to hear about their problems, and how the children cried under blankets, silently, alone.

Thea Feliks Eden's oral history stands as tribute to the memory of the Jewish children who suffered from the Nazi's genocide—those who survived and those who did not. It is also one of the few books that has been published on the Kindertransport program and one of even fewer that document the experiences of those deported to Zbaszyn, Poland on October 28, 1938. Some historical background is necessary for those readers less familiar with these events of the Holocaust.

Since her mother was originally from Poland, (her father was dead by the time the Nazis rose to power in 1933) Thea and her three brothers were considered Polish nationals, even though they were born in Germany. "Foreign" Jews were one of the first groups to be singled out for persecution. On October 6, 1938 the Polish government issued a decree invalidating the Polish passports of persons originally born in Poland who had lived out of the country for more than five years. Thus these immigrants could not return to Poland. On October 27 and 28 the Nazis began arresting Jews of Polish nationality in order to expel them. The Felix[3] family and seventeen thousand other people became stateless refugees.

On those October days, seventeen thousand men, women, and children were torn from their houses, given no time to pack belongings or arrange their affairs. They were allowed to bring ten reichsmarks per person (about $4.00). Some were deported by train or van (as Eden describes) and many arrived on foot. Upon their arrival at the border between Poland and Germany, the terrified and freezing refugees were chased through the forest by Germans with guns. Many elderly people died en route. Some people committed suicide.

The refugees were pushed across the border into the no-man's-land between Poland and Germany. After several days of chaos during which they sat in a field in heavy rain, without food or water, the Polish government agreed to put the refugees in some abandoned horse stalls near the town of Zbaszyn, Poland. On October 30 they received some assistance from Warsaw, supplied by Emanuel Ringelblum and Yitzhak Gitterman of the Joint Distribution Committee. Several days later on November 4, 1938 this committee reformed as the General (Jewish) Aid Committee for Jewish Refugees from Poland. The committee set up rudimentary field kitchens and tried to organize cultural activities for the refugees. A few individuals who had money or connections left Zbaszyn for other places in Poland, but the vast majority had no resources and stayed. The camp was finally disbanded in August, 1939 when war broke out.

Worldwide attention briefly focused on the Jews of Zbaszyn. Significant to this manuscript, one article in *The Times* of London ("Polish Jews' Expulsion—Refugees Despoiled in Germany," 3 November 1938) noted that "The deportees include more than 2000 children. . . . Disease has broken out, especially among the children."[4]

Among those interned at Zbaszyn was the Grynszpan family from Hanover, Germany. Their son, Herschel, was living in Paris at the time. After receiving a postcard from his sister Esther telling of the family's plight, Herschel, an angry youth of 17, bought a gun, went to the German embassy and shot the first official of importance he was able to see, Ernest vom Rath, the third secretary of the German embassy. The next day vom Rath died from the wounds he received. This assassination was officially presented by the Nazis as the provocation and justification for the massive violence of Kristallnacht on November 9, 1938. In one night hundreds of synagogues were burned, thousands of Jewish businesses were destroyed, their windows shattered in a rain of plate glass. This shattered glass littering the streets of Germany gave the pogrom its name, Crystal Night, or Night of the Broken Glass. Hundreds of Jews across Germany were beaten and about 30,000 were arrested and deported to concentration camps.[5]

Kristallnacht was the first large-scale organized violent pogrom against Jews carried out by the Nazi regime, and the first one accompanied by mass deportation. It represented a devastating turning point in the escalation of the Holocaust. The connection between Zbaszyn and Kristallnacht must not be forgotten.

On August 25, 1939, her thirteenth birthday, Thea finally left Zbaszyn as one of the children rescued by the Kindertransport program. She was one of almost 10,000 children saved from Germany in this way. My mother and her sister were also among those children. The Kindertransport program was organized by the British organization, The World Movement for the Care of Children from Germany. It began as a response to the pogrom of Kristallnacht and continued through the subsequent escalation of the Nazi's genocidal program. The organization was begun by Gertrude Wijsmuller-Meyer, a Dutch social worker. In December, 1938 she took a train from Holland to Vienna to meet Adolf Eichmann, chief architect of the Nazi plan to exterminate the Jews. The Nazis arrested and imprisoned her. Fearless, she still insisted on obtaining Eichmann's authorization to release 10,000 children to go to England. He mocked her and would not believe that she was not Jewish. He sexually harassed her by asking that she remove her shoes and lift her dress. Finally he agreed to let 600 children (*kinder*) go that coming Saturday.[6] The World Movement for the Care of Children from Germany arranged for the placement of German-Jewish children in English homes. While some of the children brought under Kindertransport came to live with relatives or friends (like my mother and her sister), the majority were "non-guaranteed," sponsored directly by the organization, which was supposed to make sure their needs were met.

The World Movement for the Care of Children maintained a list with descriptions and photos of Jewish children in Germany in need of rescue. They compiled this list from names sent by local Jewish refugee committees across Germany. These committees arranged for permits through the British Home Office and negotiated with the German police for each child's release from Germany. Children were brought on special Kindertransport trains across the continent and then on boats into England at Harwich, although this route varied as war spread. The first transport arrived at Harwich on December 2, 1938, and the last when war broke out on September 3, 1939. By the end of the Kindertransport, 9,254 children had been brought to England, of whom 7,482 were Jewish. These 7,482 German

Jewish children were saved from the genocide which murdered 6 million European Jews, 1.5 million of whom were children.[7]

To this day, many of the people who came to England as part of the Kindertransport program share a special bond. A newsletter, *Reunion of Kindertransport*, continues to be published in England. For many years periodic reunions of *Kinder* have been held all over the world. The most recent international reunion of over one thousand *Kinder* in England was held on June 25, 1989, and was organized by Bertha Leverton. Eden refers to this reunion in her oral history, expressing her profound disappointment that her health prevented her from attending. 1992 saw the publication of a comprehensive compilation of memoirs by members of the Kindertransports, *I Came Alone: The Stories of the Kindertransport* edited by Bertha Leverton and Shmuel Lowensohn.[8] The book is dedicated to "the memory of all the parents who made the supreme sacrifice of sending their children away never to see them again. It was not in vain; we have started a new generation again and enhanced the re-birth of the Jewish people." A special Kinderforest planted in honor of the *Kinder* now stands along the main road to Jerusalem in Israel with a commemorative plaque in English and Hebrew set in a big boulder visible from the road.

As this book goes to press, over a million refugees, many of them children, are homeless and wandering across the globe—in Bosnia, in Rwanda, in Latin America, in the Middle East, in the United States. Here in California, as elsewhere, racism and antisemitism are intensifying; the politics of fear and scapegoating are once again being promoted as an antidote to hard economic times. In this climate, the insights and experiences described in Thea Feliks Eden's oral history seem all too relevant. A whole new generation of survivors and children of survivors walks the earth, while the past still lives in the hearts and minds of those who were there, and in those who take time to listen, to read these words.

—*Irene Reti, January 1995*

Personal Introduction

I met Thea Feliks Eden in 1988 through my companion, Valerie Chase. Thea's daughter, Ilana, was playing in a musical production in San Francisco and Valerie and I drove up from Santa Cruz to visit her. The same weekend Thea also came to visit her daughter. We all had dinner in Mill Valley, at the home where Ilana was staying. I remember feeling immediately drawn to Thea, to this small composed woman with gorgeous reddish brown hair piled up on her head. The moment I heard her speak, her voice with its braid of British and German inflections electrified me, washed over me like family, familiar, so similar to the voices of my mother and aunt, also born in Germany, also Holocaust refugees.

I knew Thea was a Holocaust refugee because Valerie had told me this, but I was not prepared for the intense feelings her presence inspired in me. Thea was about my mother's height and size, and she had the same wild long brown curls unusual in women in their early sixties. I remember standing next to Thea in that kitchen in Mill Valley, shaking her hand, desperately wanting her to like me, wanting to tell her how much she reminded me of my own mother, but not wanting to invade her reserve. Besides feeling electrified, my strongest memory of that evening is of all of us sitting around after dinner in the living room playing with a package of plastic P4 polymer globules designed to help house plants stay moist. The globules swell up and retain water. They were new on the market and quite a novelty. We spent half the evening dumping slippery blobs into larger and larger water glasses, seeing how much bigger they would swell, laughing like maniacs. I especially remember Thea's laugh, a wicked, throaty, extended laugh that burst through her British reserve—the laugh of an escape artist.

What I didn't know that night in Marin County was that that meeting would be the only time I would see Thea completely well.

Shortly after her return home to Santa Barbara she began to experience the strange dizziness and weakness which eventually developed into the paralysis which afflicted her until her death from breast cancer on May 6, 1994. But my wish was granted: I did get to know Thea much better over the next six years. Valerie and I went to visit her in Santa Barbara many times. In the early years when Thea could still walk, we took walks along the ocean and through the Santa Barbara Botanical Garden. I remember standing next to Thea under a small redwood tree in the Garden. She reached out to stroke the tree's soft, dark bark, and expressed her admiration for the way redwood trees survive logging and fire to sprout new growth in rings around the stumps of their ancestors. The symbolism inherent in her admiration for those survivor trees was not lost on me.

Strangely enough, I don't remember the first time I told Thea that my parents were Holocaust refugees. What I do know is that as the years passed we had many intense conversations about her life history and the parallels with my own mother's. Thea was less than a year older than my mother. Both of them were born in Germany. Both Thea and my mother were part of the Kindertransport program which rescued German Jewish children by sheltering them in England during the war. Like my mother, Thea was a feminist all her life, an outspoken, strong woman ahead of her time. Like my mother, Thea chose to have a child when she was 33, unusual at that time. But unlike my mother, who was reunited with her parents in the United States in 1940, Thea's mother, Chaya Messer, was murdered by the Nazis. Thea said goodbye to her on her 13th birthday and never saw her again, a loss which haunted her the rest of her life. My mother's parents were born in Germany, while Thea's parents, as she discusses in the oral history, were immigrants to Germany from Eastern Europe. Those Jews not born in Germany were among the first to be persecuted, which is the reason Thea, her brothers, and her mother were interned in Zbaszyn Transit Camp in October 1938.

Unlike my mother and father (also a Holocaust refugee, born in Hungary), Thea never rejected her Jewish identity. In an attempt to try to protect me from the oppression they had experienced, my parents kept their Jewishness a secret from me and my brother until my grandfather died in 1977. Thea always considered herself Jewish, although she chose carefully with whom she would share her life story.

The conversations I shared with Thea deepened my understanding of the people and history I come from—the world of Holocaust survivors, of refugees, of displaced people. But while she never felt like an American and retained her British citizenship, Thea loved the land of California: the sea, the folded chaparral-covered mountains of Santa Barbara, such an ever-present backdrop above the red-tiled roofs of the town. One of her greatest desires was to see Yosemite, and Valerie, Thea and I often dreamed of how we would travel there together. Even when she was paralyzed and very ill we would sit and try to figure out whether she could make a trip there in the van she had had specially designed for herself to take trips in a wheelchair. I am very sad that we never made it there together, to stand under Yosemite falls and feel the spray on our faces, to watch the sunset illuminate Half Dome over the Merced River. Each time I go to Yosemite I will think of her.

In 1989 I began working as an editorial assistant for the Regional History Project at the University Library, University of California, Santa Cruz. Surrounded by bound volumes preserving the life stories of unique individuals, it seemed a natural idea to want to record Thea's life in this way. Valerie and I brought this idea to Thea and she agreed to participate. She felt it was important to document the history of the Holocaust, particularly what happened to the children, a story which has not often been told. On October 14, 1989 we went to Santa Barbara, California for the weekend and conducted a series of interviews with Thea. She was living at a rehabilitation center, the first of a series of institutions she would endure throughout her illness. Thea often remarked caustically that we could do a whole other oral history documenting the story of her battle with the health care industry, a battle strewn with the debris of countless bureaucratic forms and telephone calls, her struggle to receive home health care, insurance coverage, to seek alternative treatments and a diagnosis for her mysterious paralysis— another battle for survival.

We conducted the interviews in the lounge, until other patients would come in to watch television, at which point we would wheel Thea out to the patio under the mountains and continue talking in quiet voices, not feeling safe about other people overhearing us. Though she was in pain, Thea spoke for hours that weekend. We witnessed her life story. I was soaked in sweat, again electrified.

I went home from the interviews and dreamt all that week about the war, something that often happens to me, and other children of Holocaust survivors, displaced in our sleep, transported back fifty years. I often dream of Thea, even now after her death. Our connection seems to me paradoxical—filled with the words of rational, intellectual conversation, but also subterranean, dream-like. When we sat together I often felt pulled by the undertow of an immense unspoken shared grief, a grief too large for tears, a grief which sometimes left me exhausted.

Three days after the interviews, my town of Santa Cruz, California was rocked by a 7.1 earthquake. I remember, immersed in thoughts of the war as I was, that the earthquake seemed completely ordinary, buildings crumbling, the disruption almost comforting. While the aftershocks persisted over the next six months I transcribed the interviews on my Macintosh. Sporadically Valerie and I would hear from Thea, and she would describe her struggle to find out why she was ill. The next time we visited we brought the oral history and left it with Thea. She went over it carefully for accuracy and added a few amendments for clarity. For although Thea never had a formal college education, she was an independent scholar committed to historical accuracy. We also worked together on a series of short narratives extracted from the oral history, one of which, "Churchill and Onions" was published in the anthology *Word of Mouth*, edited by Irene Zahava.[9] I was very pleased that the story was published, and after that Thea and I spoke a number of times about her desire to write and publish more stories. The challenges of her illness made this impossible, and I think it is one of the great tragedies of Thea's life that her stunning ability with words, both in terms of speaking and writing, never found a more public forum. Those of us who knew her will always remember this quality—her wit, her capacity to tell a good story, her incisive, analytical insight. I am happy that Thea, Valerie, and I completed this oral history project together, and that at least this volume will exist as a tribute to a remarkable woman who survived one of the most horrendous chapters of human history, survived with humor and warmth, a passion for the earth's landscape, a clear and brilliant mind.

—*Irene Reti, January 1995*

Personal Introduction
and an Overview of Thea Feliks Eden's Life

In 1977 I met Thea Feliks Eden and her husband Dan through their daughter Ilana. Ilana and I played together in a string quartet group, and the Edens were generous enough to let this beginning ensemble rehearse at their house. Within the first year of knowing Thea I began to converse with her and we formed a friendship independent of the one I had with her daughter. I was twenty years old and felt like I had had a provincial Santa Barbara upbringing. Thea was one of the first people in my life to treat me as an adult. We spent hours discussing feminism, politics, philosophy, or any other subject that came up. Her wealth of experience and knowledge about many countries made her a fascinating conversationalist. Thea never missed a chance to walk and talk about what was currently on her mind.

On various occasions, Thea described her personal experience as a Jewish child who had been saved from Hitler's concentration camps by being put on a Kindertransport to England. Over the course of the next twelve years, I heard bits and pieces of various incidents from that chapter of Thea's life. As painful as these memories were, Thea was willing to share her stories and feelings with me as a family friend, realizing that because I was part Cahuilla Indian, we were both from groups that had suffered at the hands of Christian/Western culture. In spite of being an avid conversationalist, Thea was a reserved person, and not even her daughter has all the facts about her life from World War II up until the Edens settled in California. The following is a brief account of known events in Thea Feliks Eden's life after the Kindertransport years.

During World War II in England, Thea Feliks met Daniel Eden, an airplane mechanic in the British Royal Air Force. After World

War II, Thea and Dan married and lived in the newly formed state of Israel. Thea worked in the evolving Israeli banking system. Dan was involved with the formation of what became El Al, the Israeli airline. Thea was fluent in German, French, English, and Hebrew, and worked as both a translator and editorial assistant for a variety of journals. Thea's feminist views were largely shaped by the harsh reality of the attitudes toward working women that she encountered in the post-World War II economy. Although she wrote and edited for various journals, the men she worked for were unwilling to give her credit and promote her.

In the mid-1950's and early 1960's Thea's husband, Dan, was involved with deep-sea-diving research for Edwin Link.[10] During this period, the nature of Dan's work meant that the Edens lived in various Mediterranean countries. Their daughter Ilana Sharon was born in 1959 in Israel. In 1963 the Edens came to the United States. They settled in Santa Barbara, California because Dan was hired by Ocean Systems. The Edens arrived in Santa Barbara in September 1964, during the infamous and destructive Coyote Fire.

Later the Edens decided to open an antique furniture business, and went on to restoring houses. Thea and Dan were an excellent team. Thea's practical and creative sensibilities combined with Dan's mechanical mastery transformed the houses they bought and restored.

The Eden residence in Santa Barbara was always a house filled with lively debates about current events. Their daughter Ilana, a talented musician and conductor, brought an outrageous assortment of musical endeavors and friends into her parents' lives.

After Dan Eden's death in 1985, Thea was in the process of considering what direction her life might take, when she became weakened by a neurological disease which slowly began to paralyze her. No conclusive diagnosis was ever reached but the doctors thought there was the strong possibility that Thea's paralysis was in part a result of Post-Traumatic Stress Disorder resulting from her experience as a child in the Holocaust. All the survival skills that Thea had acquired as a Kindertransport child came to the front as she fought the medical establishment. Thea never wanted to be a part of any system that desensitized people and stripped them of their humanity. It was her wish not to be placed in a rest home or hospital despite the serious state of her declining health. Though she was for a time forced to reside in a convalescent hospital, she was determined to return to her home and live as independently as possible. Thea and her daughter Ilana were able to set up and keep in place an in-home health care system that continually amazed Hospice and medical professionals. In 1993 Thea developed breast cancer and she died in her Santa Barbara home on May 6, 1994.

I always felt that at some point Thea's experiences during the Holocaust needed to be documented. When her health became precarious, the urgency of this task became clear. This oral history is the story that Thea felt compelled to remember and record before she died. This project could not have taken place if my companion, Irene Reti, who met Thea in 1988, had not entered her life. Irene, as a daughter of two Holocaust survivors, was able to reach across Thea's personal reserve to ask the questions needed to record Thea's history, to bridge two Jewish generations' understanding and knowledge of the Holocaust.

Thea wanted her oral history to be a reminder that the violence war creates forever alters the lives of the children who live through the disruption, chaos, and pain that destroys their childhoods. Thea's ability to not only live through such a horrendous situation, but to remember her experiences and be able to tell her story was remarkable.

— Valerie Jean Chase, January 1995

The Oral History
of
Thea Feliks Eden

Leopold and Thea Feliks, Zbaszyn, Poland, 1939

15

Early Life in Cologne, Germany 1926-1938

Cologne really was a pretty nice town. It's on the river Rhine; it has a very famous cathedral, probably one of the most famous cathedrals in the world.[11] I remember it as a child. It was so tall. I remember standing in front of it, this tiny little kid standing in front of it, looking up. It was so, so tall . . . it [looked like] it was leaning . . . that's how tall it looked from the perspective of a child's eye. There was an area near there that I really liked, where they had some very interesting sculptures, like the seven dwarfs, stuff like that. I don't know if it was the seven dwarfs, but I remember walking in that area and just being entranced with the sculptures, and looking at the Rhine, and that was very beautiful too. So actually there are some very great memories of that particular area of the town near the Rhine that really have nothing to do with . . . nasty associations.

That was a time when you could still see beer barrels being delivered by big dray horses, and them rolling the barrels down, and also coal being delivered into the cellars from the street, anthracite and stuff—they opened the grates and they either rolled down barrels or delivered coal. I still remember a horse and carriage on special occasions, all dressed up with fringes. And I remember when the first cars came in with the built-in lights, not sticking out, but sort of in one piece. And looking, "Oh my gosh, look at this!" That was all in the early thirties.

But our house had electricity. We were high-mod. (Laughter) It was a middle-class area. Funny enough, years later in England I lived in a couple of places where they still had gas. But Cologne was a modern city. It was a cosmopolitan city, beautifully located. That whole area, the Rhine area, has lots of castles. You can go down and take a river trip. They always talk about the women luring the men to the rocks, the Lorelei. (Laughter) Do you remember that poem? Somehow it's not the fisherman who doesn't do his business right, it's the lady who's drawing him to the rocks and destruction. (Laughter) I think it was also a tourist town, to a large extent. It was a pretty busy industrial area, but nice too.

My parents had lived there at least since about 1920, maybe before. Neither of them were born in Germany, so I don't know exactly when they came there. My father was Austrian. He had been in the Austrian Army. He was on the wrong side in the First World War, irony of ironies. My mother came from a place called Galicia which changed hands every Tuesday and Thursday. I don't know what it happened to be at the time when she was born, but it used to be part of the Austro-Hungarian empire. I don't know what [country] it was the particular year she was born, because I don't know what year she was born. That's where they came from—Eastern Europe. They weren't from Germany originally.

I suspect my father, Samuel Felix, didn't come from a religious background. I just don't think he did. My mother came from a more religious background, more traditional, although she herself was not religious. I guess if she married my father she couldn't have been that religious. She just was traditional. She would go to Yom Kippur service and she'd light candles on Friday night, and that was it. I don't remember any strong religious influences at all.

I went to Temple on those High Holidays as kind of like an insurance policy. (Laughter) You go just in case there's something in it. (Laughter) I still identify with that notion. I can understand people saying, well, just in case. I think that's why a lot of people have affiliations with churches. I'm not convinced that they are so convinced about everything that they do, or that they live their lives in the manner in which they theoretically think they live them but . . . (laughter) I've never taken it terribly seriously. I think people have their own way of working out something in their mind. But with me it's much more being in tune with nature than artificial settings and buildings. I can't really identify with that, people believing they have the truth. I think maybe we all have a little glimpse of the truth now and again, but not more than that. I can't work up any enthusiasm for very strong frames.

What else can I tell you about my parents? Not much. My father died when I was so young. I was only six. He was much, much too old for my mother. It wasn't an arranged marriage. No, I don't think she would have stood for that. She was much too much of a rebel, my mother. I know that he was much older. He was probably old enough to be her father. I would guess that he was at least twenty years older. I remember my father as a much, much older man. I remember them walking arm and arm in the park and saw some compatibility there. I don't remember any sort of arguments or harshness. But, not my cup of tea in the least. I think, bad mistake when you have those age differences. But they were very common at the time. I don't look at most of those marriages as having been great marriages. That's probably true today too. So nothing much has changed. Except that there are more choices today for women, and there were less then. Perhaps there was something he could offer her, but I'm not aware of that. In any case it's not something I know much about because I was just too young.

I don't really remember much about my father. I don't remember anything positive or negative. I remember climbing up on his lap and really getting not much of any response—no rejection, but no acceptance either. It was kind of . . . oh yeah. Oh, yeah, you're here. He was a business man, pretty successful, I think, in his own way. I think originally he had some engineering background, but I'm really not sure about that either. He must have done fairly well. We had a big house, at one time anyway.

My mother was like all the people in our family, artistic in one way or another. She designed hats at one time, did some designing work, millinery. She also at one time had a store of her own, I think a fur shop. This was at a time when it wasn't that fashionable for women to have their own businesses. So in her own way, I suspect that she wasn't really content to sit at home. I think we had some staff early on, some maids, and she took herself off to some interests of her own. That might have been the business she started. As to what happened to it and how it ended, I don't know. Again, it was all over by the time I was six because he was dead and that was no longer in place. Whatever happened there I don't really know much about. I do remember having somebody else look after me as a baby, vaguely, but that's about it.

My mother's first name was Chaya. Her maiden name was Messer. Actually Messer means knife. (Laughter) Mack the Knife. My family's name was Feliks. With a "ks." Oh well, actually some of them wrote it with an "x." So who knows? They were probably being rebellious again. I think the Polish version is probably "ks" and the German version is "x" so . . . I used "ks." My father used "x." Well, we had choices, you see, when we came to England. It's like the immigrants who came to the United States, and they had an official who couldn't understand them and put down something, and (laughter) that's what you're stuck with for the next sixty years. A lot of them were simplified or changed. Nobody took that stuff too seriously either.

My mother was comfortable with children, but I think she was harassed. You have to remember she had very young children when my father died in 1933. The youngest was three, the oldest was eleven. There were four of us. She was getting sick and had a lot of responsibility. Somewhere in the thirties she got tuberculosis of the lungs and she was coughing up blood.

If I had to make a guess, I'd say she was born around 1896, or 1898. But she was pretty young. I'd say she was in her late twenties, or at the most thirty, when I was born. She was a pretty young woman.

I think my mother spoke Yiddish. But she also spoke German.

She spoke German, Polish, and I think some Yiddish. Not terribly well. I know we didn't learn it. I subsequently learned it many, many years later, after a fashion, in Israel, because I was interested. My aunt by marriage, her mother only spoke Yiddish, and she was a very nice lady. She used to read Yiddish books. By that time I'd learned Hebrew and I wanted to be able to figure out if I could also learn Yiddish. That was something that I struggled with. I never really mastered it, but to the extent that I did learn it, I gave a lot of joy. So, I was kind of proud of myself, because it was quite difficult for me. Just being able to puzzle it out, the same as you would after two or three years of high school French. You know you could puzzle it out, and say, "Oh yeah, well that's nice." As a matter of fact I did it in New York a couple of years ago. (Laughter) I was at it again. Can I do this still? Yes. Slowly. So I got a kick out of that. But it wasn't part of my background. Not really. We were German-speaking kids. And my mother spoke Polish, because in Galicia that's what you spoke. But they also lived in Austria, I'm not exactly sure how many years they spent where. But that's what she was comfortable with.

I'm the youngest now. There were four children. My oldest brother was called Heinrich. But nobody calls him Heinrich; he's really Henry and has been for years. He is four years older, I think. The second one is one year older. He was called Karol, and is called Charles now. I was called Thea with a hard T, but most people say Thea, because Theodora, or Dorthea. It's really Greek. I'm the third child and the youngest one was four years younger than I. The one who was executed was called Leopold. We called him "Poldie."

The Rise of Nazism

I don't remember anti-semitic incidents before 1933. You have to remember I was only six, well, I guess seven, in 1933. Pretty young to differentiate when something started. To me, it seems they were always there.

If you were in part of the town where you weren't known to be a Jewish child or a Jewish person, then the atmosphere changed dramatically because you weren't feeling threatened. Walking through the town, the smells were good, the sights were good, there were many nice things. . . . But of course that feeling disappeared once you approached your own area where you were known and could be threatened for no obvious reason that you could understand.

There were quite a few Jewish people living in Cologne. Some tended to live in certain areas, but we didn't. So there was nothing very specific about the area that singled us out. It was just that if you were known to be Jewish, if you had some Hitler Youth types or some Nazis, they would take the initiative of making you uncomfortable. If you were known to be a Jewish person then you were threatened just by virtue of the fact of [them] knowing. There were so many Nazis around that you could suddenly feel yourself in a totally different psychological frame of mind. I went to a Jewish school, so the same was true as you approached the school. Then you were running something of a gauntlet because people in that area knew that that was a Jewish school. It was a fluid situation where you sometimes felt fine, and often didn't, depending on really immaterial factors, but factors you couldn't control.

I think the worst thing I remember had to do with a paper called Der Stürmer.[12] That was full of the most ugly caricatures that you can imagine about Jews. They always had the most enormously hooked noses. They looked like monsters, just the worst kind of caricatures. You could never attack. You could never tear the papers down because they were behind some chicken wire and set back about an inch, in wooden frames. So you couldn't just get angry and tear the papers down, because they made damn certain that you couldn't. It was behind wire. So there they were. You were being attacked. You never knew anybody like that, but they were all supposed to be Jewish people. You never knew anybody who was like that. Yet you were being told that that's what you were. So those were the crazy elements. That was the one that you saw at street corners.

I think it was a bit later in the '30s that stores would have signs in the windows that said Jews not wanted here, don't come into our store. When I hear these stories now that people didn't know in the '30s what was going on, I say hogwash. You only had to look at the signs and the papers at every street corner to know what was going on. Every child knew. If you weren't blind, deaf and dumb you knew what was going on. That simple. At the same time, if you were away from the danger zone you could feel okay. There were nice gardens. Again, [you were fine] unless you were in a part where people knew that you were Jewish and decided to harass you on that basis.

There were psychological reasons why it was very difficult. For instance, during the '30s they had a lot of parades. They were always parading something. If somebody knew you were Jewish and you were caught in a situation where there was a parade going on, you would have to say Heil Hitler. Well if you said Heil Hitler, they'd get you for saying Heil Hitler. How dare you take the name of, even mention the name of our Führer? And if you didn't say Heil Hitler you were being disrespectful and they got you anyway. It was a Catch 22 situation—no matter what you did you were going to get it. So what basically happened was the avoidance syndrome, you started to look—was there going to be a parade, was there going to be anything going on? If there was, you ran the other way in order to avoid having to deal with a problem which you couldn't deal with satisfactorily. Because whatever you were going to do was going to be wrong.

As far as being near your own house was concerned, you got

scared. Because it would be somebody's idea of a joke to hide in the doorway and catch you as you were trying to get into your house. So you either wet your pants in a panic, or wiggled like a frightened fish. The idea was to terrify a child. That was some people's idea of fun. I experienced that a number of times. They used to have these bells in the house that you'd ring upstairs in order to open the lower door. So you'd ring your bell. And then you'd be frightened to go through the wall, because something weird might be going on.

We had a Nazi living in our house. It was a four-story house, and on one of the floors was a Nazi, a nasty piece of goods. After my father died my mother was left to support four children. So instead of having that whole big house to ourselves we kept one floor [and rented the rest]. It was a four-story building, a big house. Those times, they had big houses. It wasn't that uncommon.

What I remember is going to school and being outraged by certain things, like having to go past a certain statue of Christ, with extended arms nailed to the cross. Having heard things like that we were Christ killers, I looked at this thing on the wall, this piece of sculpture, and thought, "Christ killers? What have I got to do with that thing on the wall? What have I got to do with that? Nothing. But these people are attacking me in the street."

It's just craziness. We were supposed to be the evil ones? We weren't doing a thing. We were trying to go to school and being confronted by these images. We were being physically attacked, sometimes in the most frightening, gory ways. See this scar on my face? That was a stone arbitrarily thrown at a child, who had done nothing. And I at the time, because the blood was streaming from my face, believed that my eye was running out into my hand, because I was looking down and everything was full of blood. I had done nothing. I was standing in front of my house. From a child's perspective you have this craziness, "Here, you're the Christ killer!"

24

You get your eye practically knocked out. They missed by a tiny fraction of an inch. This is so close. Look at that scar. Then they really would have gotten me.

The craziness, there's no end to it, on so many different levels. What that does to a child's mind, I don't know, except that that child's mind really starts to think in terms of the whole world out there being dangerous, crazy, and evil. You're taught at home. This is one of the things that we were taught to do—keep your mouth shut. Don't say anything to anybody. What a thing to teach a child, to be secretive and not to talk to other people outside your home, not to say anything.

We didn't have any non-Jewish friends. How could you have any non-Jewish friends? You'd be saying something. You'd have to be on your guard there too. Besides, those kids denounced their own parents. That's what they were taught to do. Once you joined the Hitler Youth you were totally in allegiance to the Führer, not to your parents. Actually, originally the Germans themselves were in danger. The first Germans who actually got killed were the mental patients and they were considered undesirable. I don't know how many thousands and thousands of people were done in. But those were the first death victims of that campaign.

I don't think evil begins in a sudden enormous rush. It starts in small ways and grows. It's like water finding its way to the sea. It just grows and grows and grows and grows—if you let it. In Germany people allowed a lot of things to happen, and rationalized a lot of things. They bought a picture of somebody who said, "Well, enough poverty. We have to create jobs." That whole picture went with the post-war [World War I] period of putting Germany back on its feet economically. People avoided really looking at what was happening. In addition, I think a lot of industrialists believed they could control someone like Hitler and his groups, thought that they were basically not that intelligent, that they were basically not that threatening. So it may have been a big surprise to them too.

School started at six and you got one of those big dunce's caps, full of goodies. Yeah, there were those nice little human touches that made you think you were living among human beings.

I can't remember not being able to read. I'm sure that I must have learned at some point but I'm not sure that it was at school. I may have started before. I don't remember the books at home, but I remember lots of magazines, maybe because they weren't meant for children necessarily. I remember always reading, always curled up somewhere. It's a habit I've always had. . . . That was just something very basic. And of course also it wasn't dangerous. Not much could happen if you were reading.

Deported to Zbaszyn

We were deported from Germany, one night, about two weeks before Kristallnacht, at the end of October. Kristallnacht was on the [ninth and] tenth of November and this was on the 28th of October [1938]. They just came. They came to the houses and said, "You're leaving today, today, now. You're going to the station." There were some trains and they put the people on the trains.

A day you get up—it's like any other day. Suddenly there are Nazis at the door, and they tell you you're leaving your home, right now. You pack your suitcase and you've got to be at the station by five o'clock, or else. You have to be out of your house. You leave your house. You leave your possessions. You leave everything. I think you were allowed ten marks, whatever that was, a few dollars, and you're shoved on a train. You don't know where you are going. On that train they lock the doors. It's full of Jews, being sent somewhere. Somewhere along the line they stop that train and start calling out names in a certain tone of voice which means doom for somebody. You know when I think about it later, it was clearly people who had some sort of jewelry store or were taking something more than a few marks with them [that got called]. I remember the tone, the names being called.

We were all together in the same compartment. My mother even managed to think about taking some food with her. She was a smart lady. I remember it was in a big black bag. (Laughter) You lived an hour at a time. It was one of those situations where you had no control at all. You didn't know where you were going. She did—as she'd done for a long time—she did the best she could. They took some pretty sick people. I remember there was a woman there . . . my mother got pretty angry trying to keep her from being stomped on physically. She was physically impaired in some way and she couldn't move. I remember somebody saying, "Yeah, four of them came to pick her up, this woman who couldn't move."

Then the train goes on and eventually, after many hours, I don't know how many hours, you arrive at this place, this railway station. There are hundreds and hundreds and hundreds of people, all upset, with their little suitcases, and some people being beaten up, you know if they're hysterical or something. Someone is getting some tea out of the bucket; I remember some buckets with tea in them. You sit on your suitcase for many hours. Then you find out where you are going to be. You start being housed in these places that essentially are unfit for human habitation. You've never seen places like that. There is a mill with the sides missing. There are some abandoned horse stalls. This is winter time.

Basically whatever you had was taken away from you—your houses, your possessions were left in place. You were taken. Then they would take your house for not having paid your taxes which you couldn't pay because you weren't there. So they made it all legal. It was legal theft. That subsequently resulted in claims being filed against the German government for the return of those stolen houses. In our case it was ironic because the particular house we lived in was bombed to the ground and if they had regarded us as good Germans, and we'd been in the house, we probably would have all been dead anyway. (Laughter) So one of life's little ironies. The house was razed. We subsequently got the ground back. The land. (Laughter)

Of course there were some people who had relatives in Poland itself, and some of those people were better off. If the relatives had any money they could channel some help. But if you'd lived in Germany, most of your roots were really there. You didn't have a support system outside that you could call on and set up something a little bit better. You were pretty much on the rocks. My mother had a brother who eventually helped us some in little ways, but that was luck. Some people were lucky, some were not.

We were not regarded as German nationals. My mother was regarded as a Polish national. Even though all four kids had been born in Germany, we were foreigners. Crazy. It's all craziness if you try to analyze this stuff. As a child it didn't make any sense. It's like the Christ killer kind of stuff—didn't make any sense as a child, didn't make any sense later on, doesn't make any sense today, either. Now today, oddly enough, if I wanted to go back to Germany, I would be entitled to go back, and probably get all kinds of privileges there, I wouldn't be at all surprised. By virtue of the fact of having been born there, and of course a lot of these laws having been thrown out. So there are some wild ironies if you want to analyze them.

My mother was always managing. The thing that kept her going was the kids. The kids had to be looked after. No matter how sick she was she still had to do that. There was not an alternative. It's like partisans in the forest. One drops, but you carry on. You may have to bury somebody, but you keep on going because you don't have an alternative. I remember when I lived in Cologne, people sending very young children across to Holland through the forests because it was so near the border. The kids had an address in their hand. It was too dangerous for adults to try and go with them. What they were really trying to do is get those kids to slip through the German lines, the border places, and get them safe in a place like Holland. If they made it, they made it. If they didn't make it, chances are they wouldn't make it at all. Parents took tremendous risks with children to try to get them into a safe position.

A lot of the things that went on in the camps to some extent I experienced when I was interned too. The most outrageous indignities that you suffered had to do with the things that are very seldom talked about. Like, how do you go to the john when there are no johns? Or no public facilities. They don't show that on TV programs, and they don't show the perceptions of children.

Zbaszyn is on the border between Germany and Poland. Well, you should have seen what we had in that camp. These were empty, dilapidated buildings that were considered unfit for human habitation. The outhouses were holes in the ground. You looked down there and there were rats. And that was the place where you had to go, because there wasn't any other place to go. There was this filth, x amount of feet down. You look down and you see beady rat eyes. You're supposed to bend over that thing and go? You have no choice. That's a horror story for a child. You know? That place had no water. There was one pump for hundreds of people, outside the building, and snow was, this high.

You had conditions that on a daily basis were just horrifying. They stuck 24 men, women and children in a little garret, a little attic, that had water leaking through it because the building had been condemned. A little of that space was taken up by these leaking containers and some stinking straw. I couldn't stay in there. I got claustrophobic. So I'd go out and sit on the stone stairs. The heat that you got was from other little bodies that were congregating and pressing against each other, and anything you could manage to get under your butt. There wasn't much, because you didn't have much in the way of clothing. It was freezing cold. There was no heating. You got sick. Some of those things I carried around with me. That's why a couple of years later I came down with TB, when I eventually got to England.

I was interned for ten months. This was not a ten day situation. This was almost a year of incredible hardship and stress and . . . you didn't have dining rooms. You got some food but it wasn't á la mode or á la carte. There was one water pump and there were several field kitchens. In the field kitchens they prepared food.

Within that little town there was an area called "no-man's-land" between Germany and Poland. There was actually a house where some people fell into such a peculiar category that they were not allowed into Poland either. They lived in this little area. You know how between borders they have about a hundred or two hundred feet of space, and there's usually a house or two in there? I remember some people being in that house and I never understood what their particular category was. They weren't allowed on either side. They were really caught in the middle, whereas most of us had been pushed across the border into this little town, this little town with these dilapidated buildings plus a lot of people who were trying to milk these refugees for every cent that they could get, for every tiny little concession that they made.

I remember my mother paying a lot of money in order to be able to use a tin bath in somebody's kitchen, so that she could clean us up physically with some warm water. Heaven knows what it cost her for this privilege. That's the kind of thing that went on at the same time that you had these dilapidated buildings where you had absolutely no facilities at all. So it's like in certain prison camps, you could buy yourself some extra food if you had some money. You could bribe guards. That happened in Vietnam. It happens everywhere. It happens in your prisons here. If you have somebody who brings some money then you can buy dope too. (Laughter)

Certainly you can buy food. There's a commissary or whatever. That always goes on, and that went on there too, in this little village.

You had the rabid Jew-haters there, too. We had somebody next to this abandoned building who spent at least six hours of her day cursing the people in this building. Unbelievable. Again, you looked at that person and you thought, "Well, what is that I've done that I deserve this?" You have no idea. You simply have no idea. You really never did anything. Except want to play like other kids. Be like other kids.

Some people tried to set up something for the kids, some kind of teaching or something. By and large the kids went wild, just left to roam. There was nothing for us to do. There was no place for us to go.

Women were giving birth in those abandoned horse stalls. There was a lot of disease. A lot of people were dying. A lot of people. And many of them died very slowly. I remember being furious with a woman for dying slowly. I had to go through from this little room where we were to get outside. I was thinking, "Well, why don't you die? Why don't you die?" She was stirring this empty bowl, totally out of her head. She had an older mother watching her who was all yellow-faced and very thin. This daughter was stirring this empty bowl and thinking she was baking a cake. She was a big woman, and she had a little girl of her own, about eight years old or so. They were all there all the time.

It seemed like it was taking a month, but it took about a week to die. It wasn't a matter of sympathy or lack of sympathy, it was just that it was a horror story that just went on and on, and on and on. There weren't any facilities to go to the bathroom and every time this poor woman had to go it was the trek down the cold steps, and the inability to do so, and the old woman trying to cope with this stuff.

So you felt that death was no longer the enemy. It became a

31

friend in many cases. Those notions all got twisted around. You wouldn't expect a child to have thoughts like that. And yet they were there because you saw people keeling over, people getting very sick. I think I had typhus. There were outbreaks of infectious diseases because of the impossibility of keeping clean. You had lice. I have wounds on my legs today, scars that resulted from that stall. I can't stand the smell of a stall to this day. I have sensitive skin. The moment that stuff touched my skin I'd start bleeding and there wasn't any way of dressing it. The only way you could do anything was to try to keep away from the contaminating agent. But you couldn't because if you tried to sit down even to be near your friends, the stuff went through your sweat pants. That's what we were wearing most of the time. You didn't have a place to wash them either. Or dry them. Every little thing became a problem. You were basically dirty, very, very dirty. People got lice, and kids were like the monkeys, picking at each other, trying to clean each other off. We used to get these combs with the thin, delousing things, and check each other to get the eggs out of our hair, so that we wouldn't have the agony of the lice.

But actually you couldn't keep yourself clean. There was no way you could keep yourself clean. It was a daily struggle. It ended up with the parents trying to cut the hair and that kind of thing. But whatever you did basically wasn't working because the basics weren't in place for most people. That camp didn't dissolve until the war started. I don't even know whether it was dissolved then or whether the Germans just marched in and finished off those who hadn't yet been disbanded. But most people I think were released to the interior at least a week before the war started, in Poland in 1939.

My mother was trying to leave Germany. But the quotas were very, very small and it was very, very difficult. The Eastern European quotas under which she would have had to go were very, very small.

And that's a burden the world has to carry. Because the whole world was guilty of closing its eyes and deliberately making those quotas so small. They could have saved millions of people. They could have saved millions of children if they'd wanted to.

They were all trying to get out, but it was very difficult. My mother's goal was to get us out. We were on a list to go to the United States. You would have to have people who would guarantee that you wouldn't fall a burden on the country. But that didn't insure that you could get there. You still had to wait your turn. Now when you're pushed across a border arbitrarily, of course you lose your turn. Subsequently there were other ways for people to get out, either legally or illegally. Some people from Germany slipped across the border into Holland. My brother got to Lithuania. Now he didn't have a visa for Lithuania, they just got to Lithuania from Poland. The details I don't know. Got to Palestine after about two years, I don't know the exact route, certainly went through Russia.

As far as the children's transports were concerned, there was some effort on the part of various groups to try to rescue some of the kids. Don't forget very few were rescued, very, very few. Some of the governments had decided they would issue x number of visas and they would accept x number of children. You registered your children to get on a children's transport. You did not stipulate that that meant that you the parent were going to go as well, or were going to get a visa. It just meant that your child was going to go.

My mother was a widow at that time, with four children and no resources that were hers to tap within the camp where there were a lot of people who did have contacts in other countries. So she was a high priority situation and I think she just worked on it to the best of her ability.

Some people had relatives in the interior of Poland. There were big families, most of whom had always lived in Poland. Maybe the person who was being deported and their children happened to twenty years earlier move to Germany. Or maybe forty years earlier, and the kids considered themselves German kids. And they were suddenly in a situation where they had been deported. But they still had a family network within Poland. Others didn't. It was a totally mixed up situation.

There were families where everybody'd been trying to get to the States for twenty years, or thirty years. Or to some other European country. But certainly not to Poland. Because Poland was a place where there was a lot of antisemitism. A lot of the little towns, the shtetls, they started disappearing or thinning out even before the war because there was a lot of [antisemitism]. If you look at the immigrants to the United States . . . a lot of those people came at the turn of the century. The people from Russia, a lot of those came at the end of the last century, following various pogroms. There were a lot of pogroms in Russia. But there was trouble in Poland too.

A lot of people from Eastern Europe took those onion boats, well you know, steerage. Steerage passage to the United States. They were very poor. They just had hopes of being able to break that cycle of oppression and poverty once they were here. Not to say that life was easy in the United States at the turn of the century. It was not! You had sweatshops and you had appalling working conditions, and you didn't have Social Security and you didn't have some of the safety nets that are in place now. And there aren't too many in place now. (Laughter) But at that time people were still trying to get away from Eastern Europe. It wasn't confined to Jewish people. It was really, "Let us go to the New World."

So certainly there were no networks for the person who was in Zbaszyn. Their relatives could be anywhere. If they were in the United States and they happened to be on good terms, then they would probably be sent enough money so they didn't have to live in one of these abandoned buildings.

If we examined the records, the actual figures, and dug back into that information, you'd be amazed how mean, closed-minded, narrow, and isolationist the views were, including this country's [the United States]. They all had choices. The choices they made were tiny gestures. They refused to admit what the situation really was, when there was no mistaking what the situation really was. The first duty was to save as many of these kids as they could. Apart from the adults, but if you're talking innocent children at this point. And the record is abysmally bad for all these places, there's just no doubt about that. There are plenty of figures to support that information. It's a shameful record. My mother certainly tried her best. But those quotas were not flexible quotas. The fact that she got three of us out, three out of four of the children is a tribute to her tenacity, her ingenuity, self-sacrifice . . . and sheer guts. My brother was only there for five months. He was the first one my mother got out. She was working non-stop trying to get the kids out of this hell-hole. She got us on all kinds of lists. She kept the youngest [Leopold] with her. She sent the strongest one out first, the in-between one, the toughest one. He really is the toughest character. She sent him out when he was twelve years old. She did the best she could, and succeeded. I think she probably could have saved herself. She knew enough in terms of language that if she'd decided to abandon the kids I think she could have saved herself. But that's really not what she was doing. She was trying to get out herself, but at the same time she was trying to get us out too. And it was a tough, tough situation. Once we'd left Germany, once we'd been pushed into that camp, you lost all your status as far as borders were concerned anyway. Because the quotas always were based on the place where you were living.

I saw my mother the last time, oddly enough, on my birthday, my 13th birthday [August 25, 1939]. My mother was really on her own. She had that struggle for years until they executed her, essentially. It took a long time to find out how that happened. For some reason I felt compelled to find out where she had died, how she had died, which may not seem terribly rational to people. What difference theoretically does it make, which concentration camp she died in, or which town she died in, or whatever? But for some reason it made a difference to me. I really needed to find out where she died. It took about twelve years to find out because the Red Cross didn't know anything after the end of the war. I just kept on asking people who had come.

I had heard through various sources that she had moved from place to place in the early forties before everybody was concentrated in the camps. I had heard that she had moved back to her original home town on the Polish-Russian border, I guess in an effort to maybe trade food and shelter for work without pay, you know, like slave labor, which is what happened, and people made use . . . the Poles were nearly as bad as the Germans, in many ways. She probably felt maybe they could make their way into Russia, which was across the river. Perhaps she felt that if she was more on familiar ground. . . . Whatever the reason that's where she was. I discovered twelve years later, by constant inquiries from a doctor who had been a doctor in that area, and probably had brought half the local population into the world, that the only people who escaped were four adult males. They had rounded up everybody else who was Jewish and just . . . shot them. That was the end of the line for them. My youngest brother, Leopold, was with her.

For some reason that was more acceptable to me to find out. Even though I knew it might have meant they weren't even dead when they fell into the pit. Even so, that was more acceptable, to know that, than to think in terms of having been turned into soap, or having had your hair cut out and stuffed in mattresses, or having your skin framed around a lampshade, or whatever . . . these barbarities that were the ultimate in moral disintegration. Even a bullet became more acceptable, which tells you something about the kind of world we live in. I don't know whether that was a compulsion, but for some reason I felt I just wanted to know. A lot of people didn't really understand why I couldn't let that go, why I needed to . . .

"You're on Your Own, Kiddo"

Kindertransport to England

Kindertransport Children, Park of Ely, England, Circa 1940

The Last Transport Out

I left the week the war broke out. In order to get to Gdynia, which was the port from which the ship was supposed to sail, we had to go through Danzig, which was a free state but occupied by the Germans; they had just moved in. It was really questionable, it was about the 27th [August 1939] when we passed through there, as to whether that train would ever get through there. If it didn't then we would have been stopped right there. But we had to go through that area in order to reach the port. That was the only possibility. We were actually on the last ship that left Gdynia. I was on the last transport. It must have been the last transport because the port was being shut down as we were leaving. By the time we got to England war had broken out.[13] I'm sure it was the last. There's a title for you, "The Last Transport Out." A week later it wouldn't have happened. It would have been too late.

It took a week because we had to go all the way around. We went from Gdynia through Scandinavian countries. Those were the chances you were constantly taking. Could you or could you not deal with this situation? And yeah, you dealt with it, because you had no alternative. It's like if your house is on fire. You can sit on the roof and wait, hoping somebody will come with a helicopter, or you can jump into a net somebody's holding out for you. But if there isn't a helicopter and all you have is the net underneath, or sometimes not even a net, you choose to jump or burn. Nobody really knows which way you're going to do it. That's how it is.

I think that one of the strangest, and perhaps most damaging things that took place was before we came to England, when we were sent from the internment camp to this, well, I called it the delousing station. The object was to get the kids into the condition where they would not be rejected by the medical personnel because they were full of sores and needed physical health treatment. But in those places they also got the kids together and taught them songs. Part of what was wrong with that whole scenery had to do with, "You're going to new places and be merry." I remember they even taught us a song. It was a little Yiddish song called, "Be Merry." The whole object was to stuff your feelings, not to talk to people about what was hurting you. "If you're not well, if you're not feeling well, don't tell me about it, be merry." In other words put a phony face on everything and don't show other people your pain, because they won't understand your pain and they won't know how to deal with it. The implication was they won't like you because they won't know how to deal with it.

We weren't sure whether that ship was going to get to England. We thought we might get sunk on the way, because the war ships were steaming out and everything was on alert. Those few days before war broke out all the ships were moving, and there was a scare for us. We must have been on the Thames by that time, just outside territorial waters of England. They had one of these ships come up, little boats, and they came aboard for a medical inspection, which in itself was ridiculous because it was much too late to send us back to wherever we'd come from. It was a state of war already. But they took off a child. It scared the living daylights out of us. The child of course, I now realize, had an infectious disease. But they took it off. I guess they took it to a hospital, but at the time that was not clear. It was just people taking children to bad places. There was that immediate assumption that something evil had happened again, even though it was a safe place that we were headed for. I remember watching this child being lowered over the side onto this little boat. Of course they took her to a hospital. But the thoughts of the children were always that somebody must be trying to do something bad.

There must have been about 96 kids in all, in that transport. I know that originally there were supposed to be a hundred and only

96 bits of paper came through, and four kids had to be arbitrarily dropped, which talk about hell on wheels for anybody making that selection.

In the transport to England, a friend of mine at the great age of 11 was in charge of looking after twins that she kind of liked. They were much younger. To them she was the big lady, the big mama. She really took a lot of responsibility for them. Some of the kids were so young that they didn't even know their names, so young that they certainly forgot every word of German that they ever knew. I knew one case where after the war it turned out that the mother was alive and three of the children were alive and each one had grown up in a different country—one in England, one in Holland, one in Belgium. There was this poor mother trying to communicate with them. They had a major language problem. The kid I knew was maybe six when she was separated from her mother. The other one was maybe even younger, in that range where you learn easily but you also forget easily. I know that she was desperately trying to learn some words in German for her mother. This was after the war. I can imagine what the mother was suffering, having three children picking up a few words here and there. So you had some of that kind of stuff going on, where with your own child, you no longer had a common language.

Arriving in England

I got to England the week the war broke out. The first thing they gave us was one of those square boxes, a gas mask. Welcome to England! Here's a gas mask. (Laughter) Actually getting to England—well that was a very strange experience, because it was the first normal place we'd been in for about a year. They took us to this hotel, a big hotel. There were telephones there. There were boxes of chocolate from people like my brother, who'd been in England

and had come to say hello. All of a sudden we saw things we hadn't seen for a year. We went from the delousing stage of a couple of weeks earlier, to the scary week's journey on the high seas when we weren't quite sure that we were going to arrive, to this fancy hotel, where there were telephones. You picked it up, heard a foreign language, and put the phone down quickly. (Laughter) There were these very clean beds, this wonderful food, and this big hall full of people who were saying things in a language you couldn't understand. But they were smiling at you.

Actually they were also looking the kids over for possible adoption. The moment we realized that, all kinds of resistances stiffened, because, "Well we have parents, we have family. We don't want to be adopted." We didn't want to be turned around and physically examined like on the block, the slaves . . . I mean that was a polite version of that. The kids really wanted to stick together. They issued us gas masks and we stayed in some private homes for a day or two, or the hotel. The first night we all stayed in this fancy hotel, and played with telephones.

We were evacuated out of the London area because they thought that was going to be dangerous. Actually nothing happened in London the first year of the war. A lot of threats, but nothing happened. There were funny things, like eating. I remember after having been evacuated maybe six weeks, staying with some people we only stayed with for two or three weeks. I got a whole boiled onion set in front of me! We were listening to a Churchillian broadcast, I still remember that voice of Churchill's, not understanding what he was saying . . . and this big white onion in front of me! (Laughter) Sauce on it and that was the only thing that was there, this big onion with some tasty sauce. It looked so grotesque! (Laughter) I was looking at this and thinking, "I don't know how to say that I don't want to eat this onion, but I don't want to eat this onion." (Laughter) Of course we had no way of expressing what we wanted to say except to push away the plate or to refuse to do what they wanted us to do. So we were upsetting them in many different ways, without meaning to. I must have given them heart attacks three times a day in different ways. It was well meant. It was just hard, in the beginning, to learn English and to make yourself understood. Of course they didn't feel they had any responsibility in the matter. It was up to us to learn English.

And so it was, but it's hard. I mean, you're a young child. We'd already been transplanted several times, and really didn't have much of a frame of reference for anything. No matter what you were talking about. But they were very kind. Like on our birthdays they overwhelmed us with all kinds of little gifts and things, which we were no longer used to. You have to remember this was coming from Christian people. So this was a totally new experience—these nice people who were clearly trying to do all kinds of nice things for us.

When I was evacuated, they first put us with some middle-class families. But we didn't really fit in. We had such a bizarre background that we sort of went from pillar to post, stay three weeks there, four weeks there. Eventually they put two of us in the home of a canon, a church canon. He was a charming man. It was a beautiful old house, maybe twenty-five, thirty rooms, a grand old home in a beautiful garden setting. We were very fortunate because we heard good English. It could have been a working-class home where very poor English was spoken. That could have done us quite a lot of harm because the way we got sent to school and given help . . . we were put in the classroom and just physically placed there and left there to sit on a bench with no help. Hence later I turned to books without any assistance. Of course that was how I started. No one helped us. They put us in a chair, said, "Sit," and then ignored us. Not because they wanted to ignore us but because the school was an evacuated makeshift school from

London and they were trying to do the best they could under very difficult circumstances. The male teachers had been called up into the service, and some retired teachers had come out of retirement in order to help. There were makeshift buildings and the whole thing was makeshift. There was no possibility of giving refugee children some special degree of attention. It was just tough, you know, learn as best you can, when you can, if you can.

So we learned as best we could. (Laughter) Which was very haphazardly, and depended on your brain power as to what you absorbed. You sat there and nobody really bothered to find out whether you could learn anything that way or not. I remember a friend of mine being attracted to Westerns because she liked horses and there were pictures of horses. She'd start taking down a book that had a live horse on it, and then try and find something that she'd find on the board or maybe identify something that she knew. It was a totally haphazard situation. No one taught us anything. Nothing. I remember being placed with a woman who spoke very little English on the theory that she spoke a little Dutch and that might be helpful because I'd been in Holland for six weeks. (Laughter) I mean some of it was funny if you look back in retrospect.

When you look back it's pretty funny stuff! But then they placed us in this canon's house and that made a lot of sense because they spoke good English. Sort of by osmosis you just absorbed a lot of things that were positive. We were there for awhile. We were bright kids, and we caught on and started learning English.

We were trying to re-establish relationships with the kids that we'd come over with, some of whom were in the area. We were constantly trying to find some. So whenever we could make our desires known we'd say we thought we had some friends in the area, couldn't we try and find them? Of course we had all kinds of persecution complexes. I remember once going to a farm and hearing the radio blare in German, and we both assumed that there was a

German spy in that house. That was the immediate assumption—how could anybody listen to a German broadcast in that area, unless there was something wrong with them?

So you had kids with some very strange notions in their heads. But you also had kids who were trying to find their little friends. We found one or two and then we tried to stick together. We tried to congregate in the same little town, but we all ended up in different places. There was the violin teacher and the Dutch lady with the turtles and beer, and then finally somebody who spoke decent English, which really helped. The unfortunate thing there was: we had settled in rather nicely and then this guy died of a heart attack, which was a tremendous shock because that was the first really stable element in a long time. And he hadn't done anything wrong except that he associated with us. It seemed as if there was something jinxed about our very existence. This man who had been so healthy and so kind, was somehow no longer there. One day he was there, we were having dinner together, and the next day he was dead.

What happened then was that his superior in the church, the Lord Bishop, he was number three in the country, actually, who lived in this eighty-room palace next to the big cathedral (laughter) in Cambridge said, "Well, bring the children to the palace." It was called the Bishop's Palace. It had eighty rooms. This friend of mine and I shared one of these enormous rooms, which was about the size of a tract house. It was enormous, with very, very thick walls. I think they started building it in the 14th century. You don't know what cold is! They used to have these stone hot water bottles, flat bottoms, with the little screw top made out of ceramics, which you filled with water. You dressed under the blankets because you'd never make it through the outside. (Laughter) The heat was terrible and the bathrooms were half a mile away. There was all this red carpeting, but you could die before you got to the bathrooms. (Laughter) The bathrooms were enormous. When I think about it now . . . you could make six out of one of those. And beautiful, you know, marbled, very, very elegant stuff. But always cold. But there were not many [bathrooms]. There were eighty rooms, but I assure you, there weren't eight bathrooms. (Laughter)

I met my husband Dan Eden casually while I was in that palace. That Bishop died too, unfortunately. They had a habit of dying, these people. It was really terrible. They turned it into a convalescent home for the RAF, the Royal Air Force, and he was there at the time. That place was so large. There was a room next to the bedroom, where they just kept the shields on the walls. I remember going in there and counting the beds after they had turned it into a ward, and there were twenty-six beds in that hall, off our bedroom, which gives you an idea of the enormous size of that place. They moved us into a cottage, what was then a gardener's cottage, near the greenhouses, which was like an ordinary house. It was just a much more natural place to be.

So that was an interesting experience. They had beautiful gardens. It was a wonderful place. They used to try and grow peaches in England, if you can believe that. They would wrap each individual peach in a white paper bag, to protect it from the frost. They'd have things like glass houses for growing tomatoes. They even had a grape arbor. You really have to be very ingenious to grow stuff like that in England. They had things like tulip trees, and little lakes, with all kinds of flowers around them, I have some photos of that, beautiful grounds. A Rolls Royce in the front, and very impressive circular staircases.

This, all within two years from lying on the floor in filthy hay. So the transition again was from middle-class to lower-working-class, to internment camp, to Rolls Royce in the front yard. (Laughter) And kids accepting it, and surviving it, and not being totally crazed by it—while not saying anything about the shoes that were hurting you because your feet had grown. Nobody was watching that closely.

The Bishop's Palace, Ely, England, Circa 1940

We were too proud to say, "Hey my feet hurt. I really need a pair of shoes that fit." Which was the other side of that. And getting sick with TB and so on. All those things started coming out, back troubles from the cold . . . the TB, that started flaring—these things they didn't take care of. . . . Then we had the desire not to stay there because we wanted to get back to the big city. We came from big cities and we wanted to go to different schools. I wasn't able to until I was declared free of TB. I had to hang in there until I was declared healthy enough.

I learned English very fast. I drove the headmistress crazy because I walked away with the English prize, first prize. She called the school together, and I can still hear her saying, "This is a disgrace. These refugee children have won the school prize in English!" But we had a powerful incentive to learn, for Pete's sake. That was really the crux of the matter. Whereas these other kids really didn't have to. But I remember her being really outraged that these refugee kids, who had missed a year's schooling anyway while they were interned, were walking away with these school prizes, which were books, essentially. (Laughter) So we did pretty well. Fortunately, as I said, it was aided by the fact that we lived with the right people and had access to books. But no formal schooling. Nothing. It was really, "Do it on your own, kiddo." That was true wherever we were. So it was also true when we came to London—"You can work in a factory and pick up pins. Or you can work in an office and try and learn something."

Then we went to London. My older brother, I guess he was sixteen at the time, maybe seventeen, he was sort of a miniature capitalist who had enough dollars to lend me enough money to get a change of clothing. At that time everything was rationed in the clothing line. I could get a job and start work. So I took a job in an office.

I think I got to London in late '41. Then the bombing started again. So we were there for a good part of the major bombing. It came in waves; there were intervals in the bombing, periods when it was pretty quiet, and then it would start up again. Pretty intensely. I went through probably a couple of thousand raids. Of course sometimes you had raids several times a day. Then the final rocketry, the V-1's and the V-2's, where there was a lot of activity. Sometimes you really thought you'd had it.

I was not too afraid of dying. I don't think that part of my experience in England left any kind of terrible mark. It had to do with being able to fight back. You didn't have the helpless feeling that the children had. It was really quite a different feeling. First of all, everybody was under attack. Secondly, everybody fought back. There was a tremendous feeling of cooperation in England. You were doing things to help all the time, to defeat the other side, so you didn't have that feeling of being caught like a rat in a trap, that whatever you did was wrong. Very much the contrary, whatever you did tended to be right, whether you were knitting a balaclava helmet for a soldier that you didn't know, or helping deliver something to somebody who needed help, or trying to do a job which helped relieve an older person in the service. All of which we did. I ran a department in a business when I was seventeen because they started giving me a lot of responsibility. A little responsibility to start with, more when they saw I could shoulder it, more, more, until they tested you.

So in a sense, particularly for girls and women, it was an opportunity, because there were all kinds of opportunities that they gave you that they never would have given you under ordinary circumstances. Just because they needed people. They entrusted me with all their payroll. I think I was not more than sixteen. That was all cash. It was a big manufacturing company, which was considered an essential business. They allowed me to do all the correspondence. They allowed me to be in charge. Not that I did it right. I mean, I couldn't really type correctly, according to the rules. But nobody cared. It all got done. I could think and that's what they were concerned about. So they just let you do whatever you were able to do. You got your training on the job.

As a matter of fact they were most indignant after the war when these restrictions lifted, and you could do what you wanted to do, and I said I was going to leave, and get a different kind of job. And God I got hauled on the carpet, you wouldn't believe it! How ungrateful I was because I got my training there. Training! They made use of me to the best of their abilities. They got as much out of it as I did, at least. But that's how that went; there was certainly no formality involved. It was a case of: do it the best way you know how to do it! You'd be amazed. And that applied to an awful lot of women. Did you see that film, *"Rosie the Riveter*?"[14] These were women who had been housewives, and they ended up putting planes together and doing a thousand different skilled jobs that they weren't supposed to be able to do. After the war they kicked us out, saying now all the men are coming back and taking these jobs back. They passed a law that they were entitled to their jobs back, and they got their jobs back. Some of us just decided to move on to other things. And we did.

There were pretty good people, wherever we were, both in London and in the countryside. Even when we were being kind of neglected, it was benign neglect, it was not deliberate. There was nothing really bad at all. Certainly they did the best they knew how to do as far as we were concerned.

There was a lot of positive stuff going on. In general, people were so helpful to each other in London, in particular during the raids, that it was amazing to me. Very little hysteria, and very little black marketing, that I ever heard about. There must have been some, but not where I was living. Real concern to just get things done. You had your little address. If you went to your job and it was bombed, well then you would do so and so. In the buses there were such interesting situations, people would chat with each other and you'd see all the little old ladies knitting socks.

You'd have a lot of tired soldiers. I remember people being very, very tired, and somebody slumping over onto somebody's shoulder. And they wouldn't move. They'd never move away, because of the realization that this was a tired person. You timed yourself. I remember being able to get very little sleep. Because of the bombing we slept in the basement, and there wasn't fresh air. The basement was full of people. It was really the dining room where they stacked about forty mattresses in the corners, and then they stacked the dining room furniture. So it was a dining room but it was also a sleeping room. And they'd have to close the shutters because of the danger of flying glass. The air in there'd get so stale from all these bodies. You'd get up in the morning; there'd be no oxygen left to breathe. Your head would be spinning. They'd have to open the back doors to get some air in. You'd be fighting, literally, to get your head clear.

So you were tired because you really didn't get any decent sleep. Of course during the night you might have several bombing attacks. That's why you were down there to begin with. You'd have your bedrooms upstairs with your beds made, but you couldn't sleep in them. Another irony, you had these enormous big glass windows. If they exploded you'd be a dead duck. So you couldn't use them. I mean there were periods when you could, but very often you couldn't.

I spent about three years of my life not having a bed. I spent the camp time and the other time. Some people slept in the underground stations, with bunk beds. Those people lived near the docks, a lot of them, which were being bombed ruthlessly all the time. So they had bunks right up against the walls, three-tiered bunks. That got so crowded, some of those places, that they would start lying in front of the bunks. Then you'd find yourself stepping off trains and there were bodies lying on the floor in sleeping bags.

People, on the one hand, were coming from the theaters. It was interesting in theaters. The noise level of the bombing would go up, and the voices of the actors would go up. But nobody would stop, and nobody would move. The performance would go on. Yeah, I remember Lawrence Olivier, that group of some of the best actors in the world—their voices would just rise, and become stronger. The bombings wouldn't stop you going to the theater. Nothing! Life went on.

So that was a very good thing about that whole time. There were a lot of normal things going on. We'd go dancing. We'd go dancing for six hours at a time. That was wonderful. You'd work your butt off. You'd fall asleep on the bus. I used to fall asleep on the bus within a minute. If I got a seat within a minute I'd be fast asleep. Only once do I remember going past my stop. I would just keep on going, go on sleeping. One and a half stops before, I'd wake up, gather my things together. You've got this internal clock.

It was really strange because on the one hand I could teach my body, because I was tired enough, I could teach my body to sleep through the stress of a bombing raid. At the same time, if somebody opened the door . . . that had a connection with my earlier childhood years. I used to have dreams of some of those stormtroopers just being able to walk through doors no matter whether you locked them or not. I used to have those dreams regularly. That kind of noise—the instant alert, the instant flash alert. I would be aware of somebody going through the door.

So that's what the body can do for you. It's sort of protective in one sense, in many senses, for danger, but also to let you sleep if you needed to. Very often, we didn't have very much time. We had full-time jobs, it took two hours to get to and from work, we were trying to get to school, and plugging away. We still went to school from seven to ten five times a week, night school. You went to school; sometimes you were so tired, you really didn't know how tired you were. I remember once realizing that I'd better stop school for a few months when I simply hadn't heard anything for three hours, when I had simply slept. (Laughter) My head had dropped and I was out like a light and hadn't heard a word, not a word. So sometimes it took that much of a jolt to tell you, well, kiddo, you've had it for now. But you accepted all of that pressure. And at that time you had to do your own laundry, which was on a Sunday morning because you didn't have much time and there were no washing machines. And you had to do your ironing because there were no synthetics, and somehow your letter writing. Everything still had to get done.

The news starting trickling through of more and more atrocities, which we knew damn well were going on, but weren't being believed by a lot of people because they really couldn't conceive of such things happening. We knew that it was true, we'd seen, we'd had lots of tastes, not as acute, but nothing was really unbelievable. There were too many confirmations from too many independent sources for us to be able to dismiss them, and of course those beliefs in certain groups among the Jewish kids, especially the refugee kids, were quite different from the population at large.

The result was, I would wager to say, that those kids cried a lot, but they cried in silence, and they cried alone. I know I did. It's a very strange thing for a child to cry quietly without a sound. I think that's what happened. Just to conform to that picture, wanting to be accepted, not wanting to rock the boat. People couldn't understand what was rocking our boats, what thoughts we had about our families, what was happening. And our friends, don't forget we all had had school friends who had been scattered and picked up, and we had lost touch with everybody.

I think that the most damaging thing that they did to those kids was that they destroyed the trust, that natural trust that children have in adults. I didn't think to tell an adult that my foot had grown, that I needed different shoes. It wasn't entirely a matter of pride; it didn't occur to me that this was something I could talk about. This extended into all areas of life. You placed burdens on yourself that should never have been placed on anybody. But those burdens were placed by adults by the messages conveyed to those children in a thousand small ways. Children pick up on signals. The signal was, "You have no rights. You suffer in silence."

A lot of things weren't really articulated, you didn't expect help, the way we were taught English, "Well these are rooms. Sit down. Learn, if you can." Nobody stopped you. Nobody actively stopped you. But nobody encouraged you either. Nobody said, "Here's Nanny and we're going to sit down, and we're going to learn piano, or we're going to learn English because that's a cultivated language." It was, "Sink or swim, kiddo. If you swim, good for you. If you sink, well, life is tough."

You got the message that there was very little for you in the way of a support system. So you grow up not expecting a support system. If there was a support system, the only people you expected it from were one or two close friends who had remained close to you by some chance. But it was a chance. Sometimes there was no one. Sometimes there would be two or three people and you counted on those people.

I have a relationship with somebody. We have absolutely nothing in common but we are still in communication. If you asked me what have we in common I couldn't come up with anything. Our views are totally different. And yet if we didn't talk for five years we could pick up the threads in two seconds flat. I had a situation with a friend of mine, she's dead now, she died at 58.[15] We were in that same place and she found out I was in California in a roundabout manner. She called me up a few years ago, and the very first time she called we talked for two hours non-stop. Non-stop! There was this thread that really had tied us together at one point in our lives. Even though she came from this very religious background. If you tried to fill half a page with what we had in common you wouldn't be able to do it. Our lives were so different. Our beliefs were so different. Yet there was this instant communication. I would imagine if I had gone to that reunion to which I was unable to go, it would have been like that: finding some people, where on the face of it you would have nothing in common, but on a very basic, deep level you would have a great deal. There were about 1200 people who came from all over the world to that reunion in England. They came from as far away as Australia, United States, from all over Europe, from Israel.

The silence was very, very bad. I think it carried over into later lives and later attitudes, because that reticence to divulge pain has a lot of ramifications. It makes you too independent in some ways. Some people, I think, it makes too dependent, because they are looking for somebody to protect them. Others it makes too independent because they're looking to not have to ever again depend on someone. I've found out since I've become so ill that that's also a terribly unhealthy thing to do. It's not a strength, not to be able to accept. You have to be able to accept as well as to give. And not to stand off to the side. It's a hard lesson, when you come from that kind of background, because your instinct is not to trust. You trust on some level. But you don't trust on a deep level. I think you lead a much happier life if you can trust more, but when you grow up in that particular way everything that grows trust in a child is constantly being smashed.

And we really didn't have good situations. The place I lived in London was not an orphanage, it was simply a place where kids without parents lived.[16] There was so much bombing going on that you would simply disappear if you lived on your own. Nobody would know. So if you weren't 21 you had to live in some kind of supervised setting. But the reality was that we were working people many of us, and we were supporting ourselves. Now we didn't totally have to support ourselves if we didn't choose to, but many of us chose to. I remember having a job that paid for my expenses and I had about half a dollar left per week. And I chose to pay the full amount until I got my first raise a few months later in order not to be beholden to this particular group of people, whom I didn't particularly respect because I thought they were kind of exploitative types. So again, more burdens placed on oneself that didn't have to be there, self-imposed. I don't know if you can say self-imposed because really if you went back far enough it was all interconnected to what had happened to us as children.

There was good reason for the thinking. When I think about it now it seems so terribly harsh. We were so harsh on ourselves. It's like forcing ourselves to go to school five times a week. We could have turned into little prostitutes at 15, or God knows what, or placed ourselves in some dependent position. Why do some people choose one way and some people choose another? I don't know. The reality was that we were very hard on ourselves, some of us. I think I was really hard on myself, without realizing it. Not enough allowances for your own weaknesses, because nobody'd made allowances. So the measurements were wrong. A little human kindness to oneself was definitely indicated but it just had been absent on so many different levels. Sheer indifference was there because people didn't understand or they didn't know, and you weren't going to explain. Part of what is wrong with the suppression of the information concerning these unaccompanied children has to do with the fact that people really didn't know and it's a busy world and there were so many excuses for all the things that went on. So many things that people don't want to look at even today, like a lot of those problems were very solvable, if there'd been a little more caring, a little more attention to the kids. Kids have very few rights in this society. The notion that a child's view might be different from an adult's view and might have some validity in a different sense didn't even occur to them.

I'd wanted to be back in London, when the people where I was staying were saying, "Well, you can always live here. You can have your nice boy, and raise a nice family. And it will be all right." Some of these people were quite offended that that wasn't a particularly attractive thought to me. I didn't care about the bombing and I didn't care that it might kill me. I wanted to be in the city. I wanted to have an opportunity to do some other things, because I was very young and I didn't have any means. Those things struck them as being strange. I guess you could say some inner force was driving me. I wouldn't care to put a label on what particular force it was. It probably was a combination of a lot of different things. But I think it had mainly to do with independence. Not being dependent. Not having to rely on a nice husband. Or a nice setting. All of which didn't seem terribly reliable.

There were so many crazy things that had gone on over so many years. We detached our heads from our hearts. There was this outer persona, who functioned well and efficiently. But there was also this hurt child who you never talked about, kept hidden. I don't think those things ever heal. How could they heal, if it's never dealt with? It's a buried thing. It's just like an ache, or a pain, or a sore that doesn't go away, but that you accept.

I think they made some study in Israel of people who had the Holocaust background. They found that even the ones who didn't have any financial worries particularly or anything else, tended to die sooner. I don't know how accurate that is, but I seem to remember, where for no apparent reason they, as a group, were dying at early ages. Where people here might live to be eighty, there they were dying off at much earlier ages. You wonder how much that has to do with hidden stress patterns that began but were not articulated. I think there was a tremendous amount of resistance to telling one's own children about some of the things that happened, putting up these walls that shouldn't have been there, but were encouraged to be there by society at large. If you talked too much about those things you were somehow given the sense that you were on forbidden territory, that you were really digging into things that had best be forgotten.

My own feeling is that it's a crime to forget them. The only way you can deal with trying to do something about a lot of the neglect and a lot of the abuse that happens to children has to do with making sure that secrets are not part of their lives, that they feel free to speak. That's a problem today. There's a lot of theories of letting children talk and listening to them. But in practice there's a lot of attempts made to stop them. It happens in lots of abuse cases, incest cases, all kinds of stuff. Often young children are threatened with: something's going to harm somebody they care about if they divulge this secret, whatever the secret is. It's that kind of thinking that's dangerous to the mental health of kids. It wasn't any different then. It's just that the circumstances were more acute, more extreme.

I think a lot of tears were shed in silence, under blankets, or in quiet corners, but not in public. I remember very, very few of those children crying or making fusses. They all sort of plugged along. But it doesn't make any sense to me to believe that it was any different from some of the things I experienced that had a lot of hidden pain. Well I know that that's true from a lot of little things that happened. I would say that that was one of the major damage factors, that kind of abuse. Physical abuse you can get over. But that kind of mental abuse where kids are put into really untenable situations, that's something else. "Be Merry." "Be Merry." Whatever the pain is, be merry. Put on that happy face. Be merry. Do a little dance routine. I think there was a musical film where there was a big contest where you had to dance for days and days for a prize, until you dropped.[17] It's the worst form, a terrible form of exploitation because it is beyond the point of exhaustion. Somehow they put a winning number in there so somebody wins in this kind of a deal. Nobody wins in this kind of a deal.

My brother [Henry] and some other kids made their way to Lithuania.[18] In some peculiar way, they flew there, no money, no nothing, probably had more to do with how much gas was in the tank than anything else. He was literally just ahead of the Germans. They were in Lithuania for awhile. He actually got in touch with me from there by writing to a school, an address he found in a book someplace, in a magazine, and asked that they try and find me, or forward this communication, and it reached me after about six months. It went through all sorts of channels, this tiny little postcard, and because it was addressed to a school they didn't throw it away. Eventually they realized by reading it I suppose, or by having somebody read it, that it was somebody trying to reach a sibling. So it was sent from place to place to place, and eventually to a refugee committee, who traced me through their files and it was sent to the school where I was. I was handed this dirty postcard six months later.

So that's how I re-established connection with my brother, who had just stumbled out of Poland with a group of other kids. It took them about two years to reach what was then Palestine. They also went through Russia, Turkey, various other countries, some of it walking, some of it taking rides, some of it working for food on farms, by a long process of just getting from A to B. A bunch of kids with maybe one or two leaders, some of them very young, some of

61

them carrying some of the younger kids, and any kind of transportation that there was, just as the refugee stories are today, you know, cattle cars, little boat rides, a lot of foot work, a lot of walking, and hard stuff, long-lasting—years 'til you reach where you are going. Then you get to a place where they don't want to let you in because of an official mandate that says, "You aren't supposed to be in here and who are you anyway?" Refugees. A lot of those kids were also smuggled into what was then Palestine onto kibbutzim. It was pretty complicated, but the kids were adaptable and somehow they made it. They made it physically. As to what happened psychologically, and eventually the memories, that's something else.

The Bombing Raids:
"People Cooperated on a Higher and Higher Level"

I didn't feel that the war in England was all that traumatic despite all the hundreds, perhaps thousands, of bad bombing raids I went through, because it wasn't a one-way street. The bombers were going the other way too. In the parks where we had our little vegetable lots to grow extra food they were firing at any enemy planes that were up there. Yes, they were dropping bombs on us. But that wasn't a one-way street either.

The aim was to break the spirit of the Londoners by saturation bombing and they certainly didn't succeed in that. The evidence of that was daily. Even when they killed the people they still didn't affect the spirit. This period in England was extraordinarily good. People just cooperated on a higher and higher level. You saw so many good things. People helped each other in incredible ways all the time. So you didn't have the feeling of, "Boy, they're breaking this country apart."

There were fortifications on the beaches. Kids helped put them up. There were the men stringing wires and fortifications along the beaches to stop troops from coming ashore. But in many ways kids were roped in to help, on different levels. From the smallest contributions, to the max that they could render. You had a sense of pulling together all the time. You didn't have that vulnerable feeling that you were a helpless pawn in somebody's hand.

Then you heard a lot of stories of tides turning and this battle being won. For a long time it was just "The Germans are marching in and taking over." There came a point when things started to change in North Africa, all over the place, where you started hearing, "They are going to lose. They are going to lose. And we're going to win." So all those feelings of helplessness just weren't there.

If you're talking about aftereffects I don't feel much in the way of aftereffects. I remember being frightened under certain circumstances, but taking practical actions to avoid [danger]. For instance, I worked in a place where there was a lot of glass. And I, being five foot nothing, found myself a little closet. When other people started running when they heard the sirens going off I would jump into this little closet, bend my knees, so I was safe from flying glass. I didn't care if there was a direct hit. If there was a direct hit you were a goner. So you were a goner. That was in the scheme of the things at the time. So you die! It wasn't that bad. But being cut to pieces like glass flying into a pound of butter, which is what your skin would be like, which I've seen, thousands of wounds from shards of glass, that's nasty stuff. A friend of mine was cut up that way. Terrible. That was very frightening. Being buried alive was frightening. So I would avoid those situations, so that couldn't occur, and not worry about the rest.

Essentially that's what I do today. I have a no-code order in that puts in place all kinds of conditions. This is an institution. If it happens, [if I'm dying] they're to let me go. Not try any fancy tricks about resuscitating me, or getting me out of a coma. I've left strict instructions about it. Then I can forget about it and concentrate on getting well, if it's possible. On some level I was doing that as a child, saying, well, I don't want to be cut up, so I'll take very good care that that doesn't happen, and not worry about the rest.

There's some funny stories associated with air raids. I remember getting a friend of mine up on a visit and it happened to be quiet except that the raids suddenly started up again while she was there. She had this new dress and the material for the dress was rationed. This was a very precious thing that she had. She had to save very hard in order to have it made. There was this sudden raid and I told her to get into the gutter. (Laughter) And she got behind a tree. To save her dress she got behind a tree! (Laughter) It might be the wrong side of the tree. You don't know where the blast is coming from. So there were some really comic elements too, to this whole story.

I remember being lost in the dark going to the theater. Of course there was a blackout, and getting out of the theater, one of the people who had to get us back to the house had a very good sense of direction, some people have extraordinary senses of direction. We got to a street corner and somehow we ended up not knowing which way we'd come from, and not being able to find these park gates that told us where we were. We were lost in the street where we lived, not realizing that we were in the wrong block, because we had failed to count the blocks. We realized that we were at the wrong house because there was a certain dip missing in the step. That's how dark it was! You had no lights and you had fog sometimes. It was really, really dark. You weren't allowed to show any light. That was like a beacon in the night. The cars had these little hoods on them. Of course nobody could just have a car. You couldn't just drive a car, unless you were a doctor or had special permission, because you couldn't just go and buy gas. You couldn't just go and buy a car because you had money. You needed to have a reason to have a car. The headlights were covered. That's why it was so dark.

There were people who didn't go out, and some—nothing would stop them. It got so bad, the traffic sometimes. I remember the conductors getting out of the buses and going with a lantern in front of the bus, because the fog was so thick. Sometimes they would get stuck completely. The combination of fog and lack of light would be so acute that traffic got stuck. It just stopped. It was very strange, during the war, how dark it got. Especially in London, where there was a lot of fog.

Charles Feliks

Henry Feliks

Israel and Beyond

Thea Feliks Eden, Israel, Circa 1948

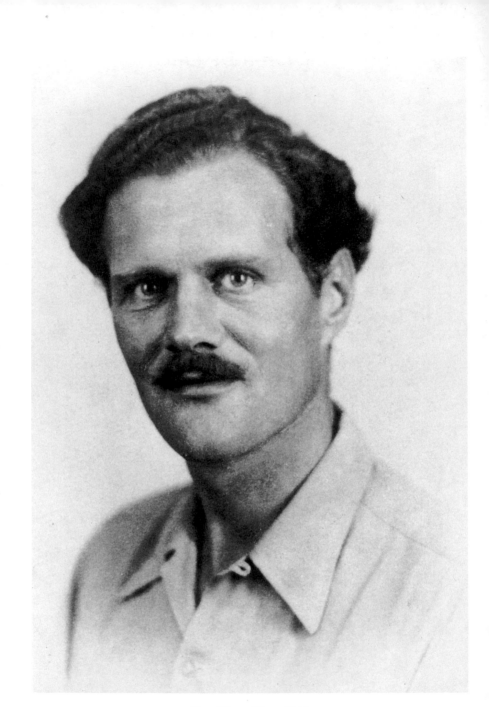

Dan Eden, Circa 1948

The Formation of Israel

[After the War] I decided that Israel was not a luxury for Jews. Israel was a necessity. Although I had no particular religious leanings, or strong feelings about that particular country, I felt that if you don't want to be persecuted you better have a country of your own, and you'd better fight for it and make sure it's there. That was part of what it meant being Jewish. It wasn't a matter of a religion. It was a matter, partly of a responsibility, and partly of something you better think about.

Don't forget what was happening at that time in that part of the world was very interesting; you had an influx of people from all over. A lot of the people who tended to go there were interesting types. It was a mix. It was an incredible time. I remember going to parties where you'd have thirty people, and twenty languages going and very, very, varied backgrounds, different reasons for being there.

My husband, for instance, had been in the Royal Air Force and had been stationed in what was then Palestine. He just decided that the whole thing was outrageous, the [British] Mandate, the way it was being dealt with.[19] Certainly the Jews had the right to have their own country. He was very willing to spend years there training people and working himself out of a job essentially, after having trained them in maintenance, of aircraft and so forth.[20] Of course they didn't have an airline. You know the famous El Al airline that is now taken for granted? At that time there was not an airline, all that had to be set in place. A lot of things had to be set in place. People came from all over the world, for various reasons, because they were interested in fostering the success of this little beleaguered country. Very often they were Jewish people who weren't particularly religious. They just had a conviction that this was something that was worthwhile doing. Just the way that there are people here who feel that spending a couple of years doing Peace Corps work makes sense, makes more sense for them in a way than for the people where they are working. It's a learning experience

It expands your horizons. Either your mind runs along those tracks or it doesn't. Some people consider it exotic or romantic, or idiotic, whatever way you want to look at it, but very often it's just a feeling that there's a certain rightness involved in doing certain things.

I took a job with what later became the National Bank of Israel.[21] I guess I was interested in the place flourishing. I wanted to be somehow connected with whatever was happening there. My brother [Henry] was living there at the time. He made his way to be safe there and joined the kibbutz. But he wanted to get out of the kibbutz. I actually got him into England. He was an artist and he fit into that scene. So I got him to England, but I had at that time been working for what was to become the National Bank. There were a lot of people in that place whose aim was to create a state. I was on the fringe of that.

A lot of people I grew up with were on the fringe of something. For example, those who were a little older than I was went to Germany after the war and acted as interpreters, or transported kids to safer areas. So they were in some way or another working with the havoc that had been caused. Some of us took kids under our wings who weren't very much younger than we were but had been in concentration camps, and had been damaged in very strange ways. I remember we had half a dozen Hungarian kids staying with us at one time, who, although the war had been over maybe a year were still hiding bread under mattresses, and bits of food in odd corners, constantly stashing things when everything was available to them that we had. The kitchens were available to them and the food—whatever we had, they had. Yet they had all these compulsions to deceive, to mislead and to hide and to stash. The wounds were very deep for some of these kids. They were people who had also lost their families. And yet they put us in separate categories because we had been, "safe" in England. "Safe." We were really not victims because we were not really in concentration camps during the war. So what did we know, really? There were these distinctions. These were distinctions that became very problematic for me.

Actually I think one of the reasons I would not have considered staying in Israel had to do with the fact that very naively I assumed that Jewish men, Israeli men would understand more accurately what it meant to be discriminated against. I found, of course, that that's a joke. They were every bit as chauvinistic as anybody else. Of course that was a very naive thought on my part, but I did have it at the time. I found exactly the same thing, with women being pushed around in the same old way. Women were given responsibility, but never credit, or very seldom credit. I worked in an organization that I left primarily because I asked some blunt questions as to why certain women who were very, very competent, and were clearly running departments, clearly didn't have the money, didn't have the title, didn't have the opportunities to advance. I was told very bluntly that because there were no laws to the contrary, that there was no room at the top for women, as there isn't today in many organizations. I said, "Well if that's what's going on I'm not sticking around." It was a naive thought at that time. Today (laughter) it would make me laugh. But at that time I really had those pipe dreams.

I was doing things like editing an economic journal that was distributed all over the world, again, in the background. You didn't get any credit for anything you did. I was doing things like cutting material out of newspapers in several languages, and reading it for management, steering it through the right courses, depending on the languages. It was kind of fun to do. I liked to read, and I could do it in the key languages. I organized a library. I tried to find work that was interesting. I wasn't necessarily rewarded. It was a compromise, as everything was, in order to function more satisfactorily. Eventually I became a freelancer because I saw that all you could end up with was being exploited one way or another.

I met some of the most interesting people I've ever met in my life in Israel. They were such a polyglot lot. A bunch of people, and so many motivations for being there, and from so many places. It was truly amazing. Sometimes the evenings you would have meeting these people would be very intense. Whether you were dancing on top of somebody's roof, or by the seashore, or in somebody's apartment, they would talk so loud and right next to you. They'd be yelling in your ear. But it was very interesting sometimes. Some of the most interesting people I've ever met I met in Israel. None of this sipping tea, and, "Oh God, let's get out of here! Can't stand any more of this chit chat." I can't stand those kinds of gatherings. Like cocktail parties.

As a country it was a pretty bare little country. Most things were supposed to be impossible and most things became possible because somebody dared to think it was possible. You had little towns springing up near impossible places where there was hardly any drinkable water. There were kibbutzim near the borders, where impossible sacrifices had to be made in order to function, and they were raising kids and animals, and taking in people in unprecedented ways. There were so few people there. It's like taking sixty million people into the United States, if anybody suggested that, even a tiny fraction of that, everybody'd throw up their hands and holler and say, "That is not feasible. That is not possible." But the fact is things are possible.

People came in so primitive, some of the Yemenites for instance, that they thought the planes that carried them there were the eagles. "You shall be carried on the wings of the eagle," or something to that effect. They would kiss the ground when they came to Israel. They'd never seen a toothbrush. You'd take the kids and stick them in the Army and there were a thousand different ways that you wouldn't think of as basic training. Amazing things went on. Tent cities went up in places where you had torrential rains. There were no buildings for them. Tents. Mud. And lack of food. I remember going to somebody's house and somebody coming from a farm with one beautiful tomato and bringing it like a crown. Look what we have!

I remember coming in from England and the biggest gifts I could bring were these two ounce containers of instant coffee. Instant coffee at that time was like the most princely gift you could give anybody. I remember somebody making a feast out of a pound of corned beef. They mixed that one pound . . . in fact it was Dan who ate it. He said, "You'd never believe it!" (Laughter) There she was, my landlady who was staying there that week. She took that one pound of corn beef and mixed it with onions and with spices and with all kinds of stuff until she had this big lump of stuff. Then she made some dough like Italian pasta and by the time she'd finished, this one pound of corn beef had been transformed into this feast for I don't know how many people. So you had people doing some incredible things with very little food, and making it tasty. They used to have these very simple meals. I remember my aunt was a dietitian and she would make something out of nothing. You had two eggs but you had a squash growing in the garden. You ground up the squash and that became part of the egg mixture with some tasty spices. It tasted very good. They were very clever in some ways.

I would say that the young Israelis had no understanding of what happened in Europe. They had been brought up in kibbutzim so they were used to fighting and carrying rifles and they really couldn't understand the older generation and what seemed to them, the lack of willingness to fight on an individual basis. I don't think they ever really understood how things were because they'd grown up free. The reality was that there was a tremendous amount of deliberate deception [during the Holocaust] like the fixtures in the

73

place where they got people to strip, supposedly to have showers when . . . the realities were very different. But beyond that they also didn't realize the physical control that can be exerted. The dogs ready to tear at you. The guns from which you couldn't escape. Generally there was a lack of understanding between the younger generation and the older. The young sabras I don't think had any clear understanding of what went on because they had always, like the situation in England, had been able to fight one way or another. So again there was too much silence.

I think there was lack of understanding. A lot of stuff went on in the ghettos. There was a lot of resistance in many different ways. But the way in which control was exerted over people was generally misunderstood, even by the young Israelis. If you don't experience it personally it's very hard to know what that kind of physical force is.

I remember dreaming that no matter what you did they could always find you. I think I mentioned the dream to you about the doors that you could lock, thick doors, and they could just push it open with a finger. They just could walk through it. Of course they had that power. In the same way they took away our houses, they took away our possessions, all they had to say, there it is. Just do it. To disempower people to that extent, to disenfranchise them to that extent—it's not something the average person can relate to. The law doesn't run that way. Unless the law is based on all these illegalities. I think that particular aspect of the story is better known because it's been dealt with by adults [survivors].

As for Palestinians, I don't know. Because Dan was not Jewish and didn't speak much Hebrew we tended to mix mostly with English-speaking people socially. Palestinians, I didn't know. That would have been more likely to happen in the rural areas because they weren't that much evident in the circles in which I moved any more than say, I don't know any Mexicans here. It's not that I have anything against Mexicans, it's just that it's just not happening. You'd have to make it happen and a lot of them wouldn't be speaking your language which would put up barriers in that sense. If they're not part of the general culture, they don't speak the language, I don't speak Arabic, so there wouldn't be much.

I didn't think of making Israel my home. It was more, "I'm glad you're here for everybody." I think it's a necessity. I don't think the world is ready for a nation without a base because that nation would become a scapegoat, no matter who it was. So I think in that sense it's just something that's everybody's business to fight for, at some level, to the extent that they can, and their conscience demands it.

I lived with non-Jews for years. I associated antisemitism with the crazy fringes which existed in England. To me they had just become crazies. I didn't associate it with the English people. Although I think there was some—there's hidden antisemitism in a lot of corners, and certainly there was in England, too. I personally experienced very little of it. So I had a mix of friends, Jewish and non-Jewish. And it didn't seem to make any difference. I ended up marrying a non-Jew, which was in itself kind of odd under the circumstances, unless I had really felt the way I just described. They were just in a different category. Yes, there were crazies. But there were a lot of people who just couldn't relate to [Nazism] any more than I could. Those years in England were pretty good years in terms of maturing, and realizing what was important and what was not important in my life.

The Choice to Have a Child

Then eventually I decided, well I might as well become a mom, because I hit 32 and Dan wanted a child. We'd been together for a long time, seven or eight years. I really didn't want a family, because I really had the feeling that I didn't want to bring children into this world. I think if he hadn't felt strongly about having a child I would never have had a child. It was only because of the constant pressure on me, the constant desire, that it eventually got through to me that here was somebody who really, really wants a child (laughter) to the point that it would be something tremendously important to him. But unless I had really been with someone who was that convinced I don't think I would have had a child. I really was convinced that it wasn't a world to bring a child into. I had the greatest doubts. It had something to do with the biological clock. At that time 32 was old to have a child. It was kind of like 5 minutes to twelve. It's not like today when you can have a child at 40 quite safely. And so I went for it. And I'm glad I did because I got such a great kid.

Yeah, I had a lot of reservations. You read the whole existential literature. It makes you wonder, that whole black way of looking at stuff, a whole range of things which you could fill a book with. I knew what I had just experienced on the job market. I thought, "Well these are my own people and they aren't any different when it comes to these basic things. Who needs it, especially if it's a girl? Why does she need to go through that?" So you have these tremendous reservations. Yet there's also that drive to have a normal life, a family. So at some point some people choose one way, some choose another. I think a lot of women had a lot of reservations. Others just plunged in and they tried to forget and tried to get somebody to protect them. They would have as many kids as possible so that they would recreate a new family. That was the other side of it. That was probably the more common way. Ones who were more introspective and more analytical, perhaps too analytical, tended to go the way I went, where it took a long time and a lot of strange thinking.

We didn't leave Israel until Ilana was nearly two. I nearly went back to England. Then at the last moment I thought, this is crazy, what's this thing with England? Dan was working in Israel at that time. Yet my instinct was to go like a homing pigeon back to England. But I really didn't have a home in England. So I ended up staying in Israel, in Tel Aviv. But I remember the hesitation, it was really like a homing pigeon, wanting to go home. It did not seem the right place to have that child. I don't think it had anything to do with the fighting in Israel. There was always trouble but I'd never known anything except trouble. So what else is new? Up to that point I'd never known any quiet sort of existence. What I considered quiet other people would have considered crazy. So it wasn't that. It was just that it seemed that the right place was England, not Israel. Physically my home was an apartment in Tel Aviv, and yet it didn't seem quite right.

It turned out not to be because we left eventually. We left less than a couple of years later and we never returned. I don't miss it. It was just like another place I'd left. But then I don't feel very strong alliances to specific places. I could move out of an apartment and a week later not tell you what color the walls were. I lived in so many places. One time I remember being asked to fill out all the places I'd lived, and I just stood and stared in amazement. How would I know? Did I have a list of addresses? How would I know? There were so many. I couldn't necessarily recall the towns, never mind the addresses.

"I Identify as More English than Anything Else"

I think I had more in common with the English because that's the first thing that felt normal to me. It's the first thing I could identify with. I really like the English language. I find it to be beautiful, very rich. Much richer than any other language. It wasn't just the literature. There were a lot of things about the people that I really liked, about the countryside that I liked. And the humor. There's something about English humor that really jibed with something in my head. I mean it makes me laugh. There's a lot of things about English humor that really I enjoy immensely. Whereas German humor is most unfunny to me. And always has been. There's very little there. And even today I can watch things on TV and it's very seldom that something will make me laugh, if it's in German. I can see what somebody might find funny, but I don't find it funny. But English humor, and some offbeat humor strikes me as hilarious, a lot of it. It's as if that came with the mother's milk. Very, very close to my thinking. I think it was the best ingredient between my husband and myself. Things would make us laugh. We would be rolling around over things that other people wouldn't think were very funny because a lot of people think English humor's not very funny. It's odd. It's quirky. And I love it. I would say to the extent that I'm anything, in terms of nationality, in my uncertain status, I would say that I would identify as more English than anything else.

I was born in Germany but there was this uncertain element. I've always been displaced. I went to Poland but I wasn't accepted as being Polish because I'd been born in Germany. I went to England—well I was a refugee child, of uncertain nationality. In fact, my passport said "uncertain" because I couldn't pinpoint my mother's date of birth. (Laughter) Consequently what she'd been. So even my passport was uncertain. (Laughter) Then when I lived in Israel, they considered me, "Oh you know, that English kid."

Well, the fact is I actually acquired a nationality. I am British. The only nationality I've ever had is, in fact, a British citizenship. I'm still a British citizen. One of the reasons why I'm reluctant to give it up is because they're the only ones who would give it to me, without any demands. It was just a special law they passed to cover these kids. I don't even remember what the law was, but I know that I was able to do it. I had been in England about twelve years by the time I did that. In fact it wasn't very long before I immigrated to start the ball rolling again. Then I was "that British one."

I don't answer the question to this day, "Where do you come from? What are you?" I don't know how to answer the question, because it's a puzzle to me. So I laugh it off. I say, "Well, of European hash." I can't say I'm German. I won't say I'm German, even though I was born there. "Where were you born?" I don't like that question. Because it implies that I'm German. And I can't say I'm German without giving an explanation, because I don't want to be mistaken for being German. I can't do that. So my way of coping with it is to just laugh it off and say, "Oh, our family is just European hash." And if I become closer to them then they hear the story. But I don't want to tell everybody the story. And I don't want to be mistaken for German. That I have an inherent dislike of. That I just can't do. If I'm pushed then I say, "Well I was born in Germany of foreign parents." I have to add that. That my parents weren't German. Now that's a compulsion I have to this day, and I will always have. I will never be able to say I'm a German citizen. Just couldn't.

I identify much more with English thinking than say, for instance, with Israeli thinking. Now you have to realize that there are many people in Israel that are not religious. There's only a tiny minority. So they are secular people. But I didn't have that much in common with them. There was an odd one here or there, but basically, I just didn't. I can't tell you why. I can only give you the facts. Maybe because I spent the formative years of my life in England, all the teen years when you really are impressionable in many different ways, and culturally I was absorbing a lot of stuff that really helped me. But that's where I always felt most comfortable.

Organized Religion

I don't go around saying I'm Jewish any more than I would say I'm Catholic or Methodist. It doesn't really mean anything to me in that sense. If somebody said something negative about Jews, I would tend to say, "Oh, really? And what do you base that on?" Then it would come out. If it comes up in a positive sense, I would probably joke about it and say something like, "Well, isn't it interesting that most good violinists are Jews?" And go back to something like the old joke and say, "Well you know, when you're running through a pogrom it's too difficult to carry a piano!" (Laughter)

I think of religion as causing trouble. As opposed to faith, which I think gives people something. Organized religion has a lot more in common with business. Not to be confused with faith. Some people have faith in a higher being and they need a frame like a house of worship to function. But that's alien to me. A house, a building to me is a confining thing. To me, faith is something larger, in the sense of a wider world, has more to do with nature. I would be much more likely to find that on top of a mountain or in a wood, than in a house of worship. A man-made building would be a confining influence because I find within that structure you usually start finding a hierarchy of people. And within that hierarchy of people you get the same kind of discrimination and nonsense that creates a lot of trouble for all of us in general.

Could Something Like the Holocaust Happen in the United States?

Do I think something like this could happen here? I think people can go backwards as well as forwards. Could they succeed? I doubt it. But could they make a damn good try? Would there be lots of people who would be willing to go along? Yes, probably.

I think that there is a herd instinct in a lot of people that is incredibly strong. You can sell them almost anything. If you can sell them some of the stuff in the supermarket . . . they'll not only pay for it, but they'll pay for it and eat it. It has fifty-seven chemicals in it, and they don't know what they are. If they thought about it they'd have to come to the conclusion that if the chemicals increase the shelf life of an item it might not be that good for their insides.

Look at the whole structure of how life is lived, at incredible cost in many directions. I think you can talk people into a great many things that don't make any sense at all. And I think there are a lot of people who are so full of inadequacies that they are forever projecting their own inadequacies onto other people and they want to blame them. It means finding scapegoats. That is a very deep trait in people.

I have always thought that all people have to have a country. You can't have a group of people like the Jewish people for centuries and centuries sort of owing allegiance to different countries. It doesn't really work. It works when things go well, but when things don't go well economically, or in some other way, then there are lots of people who are looking for scapegoats. You may have been an outsider for a hundred years or a thousand years, but at that point, when they're looking for scapegoats, you're going to be that scapegoat unless you have your own place to go to. That's how it is.

If you had a really serious depression here, and a lot of people in power who really didn't care about social programs at all, and were determined to let dog eat dog, I think you would see hate groups arise, and more and more people join them. Then if you have charismatic leaders . . . Look around the world. The evangelical preachers who we've just seen exposed as really dishonest and manipulative people—they have millions of followers who give them lots and lots of money. All you can say is that they have something about them that attracts people whose lives are rather empty, and feel they need a leader of some kind. It's a very dangerous thing.

Add to that the fact that you can buy air time, and flood the minds of a lot of people with false information, or half-true information. That happens all the time in public relations, whether

81

it's [selling] products or a point of view. I'm not sure that it makes much difference. It's a highly developed field of work these days.

Any mass communication brings with it danger, I think, in that sense. You are vulnerable unless you are pretty well informed. Well, you can say there are lots of well-informed people. But actually I'm not so sure. I think a lot of people get their information from the same source. It's not too difficult to control people, or a good number of them.

—Santa Barbara, California
October, 1989

Afterword by Ilana Eden

It is with the deepest sense of gratitude that I receive, on behalf of my mother, Thea Eden, the gift of voice bestowed upon her by writers Irene Reti and Valerie Chase. Their respect, committed involvement, and desire for accuracy make this broadcast of what had always been such a private and protected story possible. I know something of the courage it took for my mother to lower her guard, break the silence, and most of all trust another human being to handle her with care. I am especially grateful that she experienced the passing on of her story in such a positive and life-affirming way. Though we can only speculate as to what would have been unveiled if she had had more time, one lesson here is that her voice, like so many others of her time, was strong and knowing and valuable.

I too received a gift. I was given new "family." In a broad sense, I gained a palpable understanding that there are countless families like mine which were forever altered by these horrific and devastating events, and, closer to home, I experienced these two friends of mine becoming so intimately informed. They came unafraid of what they would encounter and brought with them the grace of true understanding. This project returned to me large parts of my own history. There were many experiences which were simply too painful for my mother to convey without getting swept away by her anguish. These were left with me as fragments that refused to take shape, troubling and most haunting when my mind would struggle against the *implied* scenarios that rolled by one after the other. These visions of mine rarely had endings, so coming to grips with the real story and putting it in proper perspective was not possible. In Irene's forward she speaks of feeling "pulled by the undertow of an immense unspoken shared grief." Because she felt this herself and with my mother, I feel I've been given kin who speak and feel as I do.

As the daughter of a child of the Kindertransport, I now know that it is only through fierce determination and the real hope encouraged by gifts such as these that true healing can occur.

Notes

[1] Julie Heifetz, *Too Young to Remember.* (Detroit: Wayne State University Press 1989) p. 18.

[2] For a detailed explanation of the events in Germany leading to Zbaszyn see Gerald Schwab, *The Day the Holocaust Began: The Odyssey of Herschel Grynszpan.* (New York: Praeger, 1990). See also Israel Gutman, Editor-in-Chief, *Encyclopedia of the Holocaust.* (Yad Vashem: Sifriat Poalim Publishing House, 1990).

[3] As Thea details in her oral history, her father chose to use the spelling "Felix." After her immigration to England, Thea chose to spell her name "Feliks."

[4] Schwab, p. 64.

[5] Gutman, pp. 837-838.

[6] Olga Drucker, "Kindertransport Reunion: A Personal Remembrance," *Lilith : The Jewish Women's Magazine*, pp. 4-5, Fall 1989.

[7] Karen Gershon, editor, *We Came as Children: A Collective Autobiography.* (New York: Harcourt, Brace & World, Inc. 1966).

[8] Bertha Leverton and Shmuel Lowensohn, *I Came Alone: The Stories of the Kindertransport.* (Sussex, England: The Book Guild, 1990). The organization Reunion of Kindertransport, which publishes a newsletter, can be contacted through Bertha Leverton at 9 Adamson Road, London, NW3 3HX United Kingdom.

[9] Irene Zahava, editor, *Word of Mouth 1: Short-Short Stories by 100 Women Writers.* (Freedom, CA: Crossing Press, 1991) p. 28.

[10] Dan Eden worked as an engineer for Edwin (Albert) Link (1904-1981). Link was an inventor, oceanologist and industrialist. His most famous inventions were the Link flight simulator for training pilots, and deep-sea lockout submersibles which facilitate deep sea diving, especially for archaeological research. In 1959 Link designed, *Sea Diver*, the first vessel built especially for underwater archaeology. See Marion Clayton Link, *Sea Diver.* (Coral Gables, FL. University of Miami Press, 1958), Marion Clayton Link, *Windows in the Sea.* (Washington D.C. Smithsonian Institution Press, 1973) and Susan van Hoek with Marion Clayton Link, *From Sky to Sea: A Story of Edwin A. Link.* (Flagstaff, Arizona, Best Publishing Company, 1993).

[11] Eden is probably referring to the Cologne Gothic Cathedral, constructed in 1248 by Archbishop Conrad von Hochstaden.

[12]*Der Stürmer* was a Nazi propaganda weekly newspaper published by Julius Streicher, from 1923-1945. When Hitler came to power in 1933 it was already selling twenty-five thousand copies weekly. By 1938 the newspaper reached a circulation of half a million copies a week. According to the *Encyclopedia of the Holocaust*, *Der Stürmer* was first sold by street vendors and newsstand dealers. Eventually it was advertised "by means of showcase displays put up in places where people naturally congregated—bus stops, busy streets, parks, and factory canteens. The displays were changed weekly and were protected against vandals by 'Stürmer guards'," which are probably what Eden was referring to.

[13]"We docked at the Tower Bridge. The man who welcomed us was a member of Parliament. His name was Lansbury and he made a speech. Of course we didn't understand a word of it."—Benno Katz, Conversation, January 1995. Mr. Katz was a lifelong friend of Thea Eden's. They knew each other as children since their mothers were friends. They were on the same Kindertransport to England. Both immigrated to Israel after the war and later to California.—Editors.

[14]*Life and times of Rosie the Riveter.* (Motion picture), a Clarity production; produced and directed by Connie Field. Los Angeles, CA.: Direct Cinema Ltd., 1987.

[15] The friend's last name was Laufer.—Benno Katz, Conversation, January 1995.

[16] The name of this place was Cazonove Hostel.—Benno Katz, Conversation, January 1995.

[17]*They Shoot Horses, Don't They?* Sydney Pollack (Director), 1969. Based on Horace McCoy's novel.

[18] Her brother Henry, who was a painter, moved to Canada and became a teacher. The other surviving brother, Charles, stayed in England and was a businessman.

[19] The Mandate system was established after World War I by the Treaty of Versailles for the administration of former overseas possessions of Germany and parts of the Turkish empire. The Mandate for Palestine was given to Great Britain on April 25, 1920, which was supposed to administer Palestine with recognition of "the historical connection of the Jewish people with Palestine and to the grounds for reconstituting their national home in that country." But on May 17, 1939, in fear of the Jews becoming a majority in Palestine, Great Britain issued the White Paper, which limited Jewish immigration to 75,000, which closed Palestine to Jewish refugees fleeing Nazi Europe. Geoffrey Wigodern, Editor-in-Chief, *New Standard Jewish Encyclopedia.* (Facts on File, 1992).

[20] Dan Eden worked for Bedek, the company which took care of the planes used by El Al.—Benno Katz, Conversation, January 1995.

[21] At the time the bank was called the Anglo-Palestine Bank.—Benno Katz, Conversation, January 1995.

Interview Questions

Childhood/Germany

- Can you describe Cologne?
- What was the house you grew up in like?
- What was the street like?
- What was your childhood like?
- What do you remember about your grandparents?
- Were they from Germany originally?
- Were they religious?
- Were your parents religious?
- Can you tell me as much as you feel comfortable with about your parents?
- Do you remember antisemitic incidents before 1933?
- What's the first antisemitic incident you remember?
- Were your parents trying to emigrate out of Germany?
- What avenues were they taking?
- Did you have friends that weren't Jewish as a child? Did any become Nazis?
- Where were you on Kristallnacht? What happened?

England

- How did you end up on the children's transport?
- What was the children's transport like?
- What was the general feeling among the children?
- What was the orphanage like?
- Where was it in England?
- Can you describe the building, the teachers?
- Did you feel welcome there?
- What did you eat?
- Was it a tight community?
- Was it hard to learn English?
- Did you try to become English?
- Did you experience antisemitism in England?
- How would you describe yourself during those years?
- How present was was the war?
- Were bombs dropped on that area?
- Did you feel safe there?
- How did you feel when the war was over?
- What did you do?
- Did you try to find people in your family?
- How did you meet Dan?
- Do you have contact with people you met as a teenager?

Israel

- When did you get to Israel?
- How did you get there?
- What part of Israel were you living in?
- What were you doing in Israel?
- What was Dan doing?
- What was Israel like during those years?
- What impression or opinion do you want people to know or remember about the war?
- What did you think of it as a country?
- How were survivors treated in Israel?
- Right now Israel is coming under attack for its treatment of Palestineans. Did you have any interactions with Palestineans? How did other Jews interact with Palestineans?
- What did you think of the Eichmann trial?
- Did you intend to make Israel your permanent home?

General Questions

- Would you describe yourself as being Jewish?
- How public are you about it?
- Do you tell people you are a child survivor of the Holocaust?
- What do you say when people ask, "Where are you from?"
- Do you think something like the Holocaust could happen in the United States?
- What coping mechanisms did you use to deal with the violence you experienced during the war?
- How do you think being a child affected your experience during the Holocaust?
- Do you feel like child survivors are taken less seriously than adults?
- What effects do you think the Holocaust had on your personality as an adult? On your body?
- Did your brothers react differently to the war?
- Have you talked about the war with family, friends, anyone? (Dan, Ilana) Was there anything you wanted to pass on?
- Do you think about going back to Germany?
- How would you rate contemporary Germany's response to the Holocaust?
- What impression or opinion do you want people to know or remember about the war?

Thea Feliks Eden, Santa Barbara, California
Circa 1988